Due Re...	Due R...
Date Date	

THE EQUILIBRIST

The EQUILIBRIST

A Study of John Crowe Ransom's Poems, 1916–1963

ROBERT BUFFINGTON

Nashville
VANDERBILT UNIVERSITY PRESS
1967

Acknowledgements

GRATEFUL acknowledgement is made to the following, who have granted permission for the reprinting of selections from the books and periodicals listed below:

Harcourt, Brace and World. For the selections from *God Without Thunder,* by John Crowe Ransom, copyright 1930, © 1958 by John Crowe Ransom. Used by permission of Harcourt, Brace & World, Inc.

Holt, Rinehart and Winston, Inc. For the selections from *Poems About God,* by John Crowe Ransom, copyright 1919 by Henry Holt & Co., Inc.; copyright 1947 by John Crowe Ransom. Used by permission of the author. For the selections from *Conversations on the Craft of Poetry,* a transcript of the tape recording made to accompany *Understanding Poetry,* Third Edition, by Cleanth Brooks and Robert Penn Warren. Copyright © 1961 by Holt, Rinehart and Winston, Inc. Reprinted by permission of Holt, Rinehart and Winston, Inc.

Alfred A. Knopf, Inc. For the selections from *Chills and Fever,* by John Crowe Ransom, copyright 1924 by Alfred A. Knopf, Inc.; *Two Gentlemen in Bonds,* by John Crowe Ransom, copyright 1927 by Alfred A. Knopf, Inc.; *Selected Poems: A Revised and Enlarged Edition, 1963,* by John Crowe Ransom, copyright 1924, 1927, 1934, 1939, 1945, © 1962, 1963 by Alfred A. Knopf, Inc.; "Tonio Kröger," by Thomas Mann, from *Stories of Three Decades,* translated by H. T. Lowe-Porter, copyright © 1951 by Alfred A. Knopf, Inc.

Little, Brown and Company. For the selections from "On Theodore Roethke's 'In A Dark Time'" and "And Now the Grateful Author," by John Crowe Ransom, from *The Contempo-*

rary Poet as Artist and Critic: Eight Symposia, edited by Anthony Ostroff, copyright © 1964 by Little, Brown and Company, Inc.

New Directions Publishing Corp. For the selections from *The New Criticism,* by John Crowe Ransom, copyright 1941 by New Directions Publishing Corp.

Charles Scribner's Sons. For the selections from *The World's Body,* by John Crowe Ransom, copyright 1938 by Charles Scribner's Sons.

The Viking Press, Inc. For the selections from *Women in Love,* by D. H. Lawrence (Compass Edition). Copyright by the Viking Press.

The Explicator. For the selections from "Ransom's 'Prelude to an Evening,'" by Virginia L. Peck, copyright 1962 by *The Explicator.*

The Kenyon Review. For the selections from "The Planetary Poet," by John Crowe Ransom, copyright © 1964 by Kenyon College. Copyright © 1964 by John Crowe Ransom. Used by permission of the author.

The New Republic. For the selections from "The Poems of T. S. Eliot: A Perspective," by John Crowe Ransom, copyright © 1952 by the *New Republic, Inc.* Copyright © 1952 by John Crowe Ransom. Used by permission of the author.

Perspective. For selections from "The Civilized Poetry of John Crowe Ransom," by Thomas H. Parsons, copyright 1964 by *Perspective.*

The Sewanee Review. For parts of two prose selections by John Crowe Ransom which appeared originally in the *Sewanee Review:* "On Shakespeare's Language," copyright © 1947 by the University of the South. Copyright © 1947 by John Crowe Ransom; "In Amicitia," copyright © 1959 by the University of the South. Copyright © 1950 by John Crowe Ransom. Used by permission of the author.

Equilibrists lie here; stranger, tread light . . .

Contents

THE EQUILIBRIST

| Chapter I | # Introduction |

"Study is only a serious form of gossip"
—E. M. Forster

THE most general thing to be said about John Crowe Ransom is that he is a dualist. Man, he believes, must be as content as he can with a dual citizenship, living now in one country, now in the other, never enjoying a permanent home; it is his lasting temptation, and the deadliest error, to try to renounce one or the other for the simplicity of one allegiance. This error Ransom defines historically in *God Without Thunder* as "*the moment when the Roman Church sanctioned the doctrine of Filioque*"—the doctrine of "the Man-God Christ, the closest approach to pure secularism that a religion has ever made"—and so approved the Occident's glorification of the rational and denial of the irrational. "Western empire has developed out of that choice, and Western science, and Western business."[1] In the poems the error is illustrated by the lovers ("Hilda," "Spectral Lovers") who try to resolve the unresolvable conflicts between soul and body, mind and emotion, in favor of soul or in favor of mind. And the dualism shows in the criticism in Ransom's determinedly keeping reason and emotion separate (let us take the feelings in a poem for granted, he says, and talk about what is intelligible); in his disinclination to believe in the "psychological magic" T. S. Eliot attributed to poets of the seventeenth century, the unity of thought and feeling.

1. *God Without Thunder: An Unorthodox Defense of Orthodoxy* (New York: Harcourt, Brace, 1930), pp. 167, 305.

1

That the three careers of Ransom—as poet, as critic, and as *Kulturkritiker*—run their courses about this common center (like the three legs of the triskelion, the Fugitive sign) is worth remarking in an age when most of us are "shreds and patches and old cogwheels held together with pieces of rusty barbed wire and spit and bits of string"[2] (the words are Robert Penn Warren's in a novel about the division of the age, the conflict between the man pledged to the simplicity of fact and the man pledged to the simplicity of idea). But this is a matter of *insis*tence rather than consistence on Ransom's part. He did not begin to grow conscious of the center of his thinking and give it explicit expression in his poetry until his third volume, *Two Gentlemen in Bonds* (1927), which concluded his poetic career proper and suffered a little for the consciousness. The discursive writings all followed: *God Without Thunder,* the Agrarian essays, *The World's Body, The New Criticism.*

True, in the last book, in 1941, he officially announced his withdrawal from an adamantly traditionalist position, and in the subsequent essays, some of which are reprinted in *Poems and Essays* (1955), he has expressed a new, mixed view of the modern American culture. But there has been no change in his central philosophy; the change is in his view of the kinds of society it is possible to erect upon the dual basis of man's nature. And this means a change in his view only of what he seems to regard anyway as a mere surface of the problem of being human; the poem of his that most explicitly treats a social or cultural theme, "Antique Harvesters," concludes with lines that abruptly remove our attention to the metaphysical realm, where the future of the South, the destinies of cultures and societies no longer matter. That is the realm where Ransom feels the most comfortable; and accordingly the major theme in his poetry, as in Hardy, one of his masters, is death: "the great subject of poetry, the most serious subject,"[3] he has said.

Even the change of view announced in *The New Criticism*

2. *All the King's Men* (New York: Modern Library, 1953), p. 220.
3. Cleanth Brooks *et al., Conversations on the Craft of Poetry* (New York: Holt, Rinehart and Winston, 1961), p. 21.

has been exaggerated in its degree by the liberal critic or scholar who is a little overanxious to demonstrate Ransom's conversion to his own truths. How Ransom himself would like the change to be taken may be hinted at in an essay on Wallace Stevens. Commenting on the serenity of Stevens's last book, he suddenly asks, "Had he turned into a saint?" Ransom can imagine three kinds of sainthood:

One might have consisted in an invincible benevolence; a tranquility toward the people and places and faiths he had once scorned, as if now he conceded them their equal right to be. Another might have been a pure beatitude, as when the mind achieves a childhood innocence again, and is visited by visions and angels. Or a third kind, a more official sainthood, into which a little of vanity might enter: the sense that he had been a mighty and effectual evangelist of his faith. There was something of each of these in him.[4]

An admirer of Stevens ("Prelude to an Evening" owes a little to Stevens's "Sunday Morning"), Ransom might be measuring himself for the first and third kinds, and especially for the first. Benevolence—a concession of the other side's "equal right to be"—rather than conversion, is the principle that shows most in his altered view of modern society. It developed sometime between 1936, when he published his last Agrarian essays, and 1941.

I was questioning the evidences which had led to my own personal set against the age. . . . I could not find the certain reasons for thinking the modern society was destitute of its normal humanity, and in the midst of all the confusion I began to have hopes for it, even on its own terms.[5]

But he has not gotten beyond hope; he shows no enthusiasm for the new order. And part of his hope in the beginning had nothing to do with the newness of the new; it was that what the naturalists and positivists were seeking to establish would

4. "The Planetary Poet," *The Kenyon Review*, XXVI, No. 1 (Winter, 1964), 263–264.
5. "The Poems of T. S. Eliot: A Perspective," *The New Republic*, Dec. 8, 1952, pp. 16–17.

of necessity turn out to be not very much different from the old order, after all. He wrote in *The New Criticism*:

Eliot is one of the foci of a distinguished group of literary men with whose sentiments I have always had complete sympathy; I am convinced of their rightness, but not of what I should call their righteousness; for they do not propose to have commerce with the world. . . . I have said probably nearly as much, and more than once; but increasingly now I feel that such a policy is too luxurious for my blood. The forces that have captured the world are trying to found a new civilization, and I imagine about that, first, that it is going to be much harder than they suppose to get everything into it, and, second, that when they have got a new civilization it may turn out to be oddly like the old one. . . . Almost every day they find evidences which they cannot deal with so nicely as they expected.[6]

Benevolence, as I have said, is the strongest quality that shows. More recently, recalling the Agrarian days in honor of Allen Tate, he has shown the same mixed feeling, with no stronger mixture of zeal:

We were engaged upon a war that was already lost. . . . But we were right in thinking that the times were bad, and even in thinking they were desperately bad, inasmuch as they have only worsened since.

. . . . . .

Our New Age seems to have lost those marks of a culture which go with a metaphysical taste and to have lapsed into something like a sprawling and unformed barbarism. So I have often recited Tate's position with full accord. And yet at other times in my inconclusive way I have had a small persistent hope, perhaps a forced hope, in considering that the new barbarians are of our own breed and country, our friends, perhaps even our children, and surely must be destined to erect a new culture though they will have to start all over again at the bottom to discover its new forms. I have talked about their potential, and watched for and sometimes approved a few cultural signs as they appeared. That was an anthropological line of my own; Tate has known it of me and suffered it. And my hope is not likely to be justified in my time nor even in his.[7]

6. Norfolk, Conn.: New Directions, 1941, pp. 200–201.
7. "In Amicitia," *The Sewanee Review*, LXVII, No. 4 (Autumn, 1959), 534, 536–537.

It is clear from his "Emperics in Politics" (*Poems and Essays*), where he is careful to refer to the conservatives as "they," that he presently wishes to be taken as a liberal; but it is equally clear from "The Communities of Letters," in the same volume, where he is careful to refer to the liberals as "they," that he means to dissociate himself from the busier exercises of liberalism. If he is a liberal, he is of a very eclectic kind, and with above all the distinction that Lionel Trilling has defined in E. M. Forster: freedom from the error of assuming that humankind someday will develop inconceivable virtues.

In comparing Ransom with Forster we see in just what his modernity consists.[8] (Ransom is an admirer of Forster too: he wrote a brief appreciation of him for the *Kenyon Review* to observe his revival in America during the second world war.) Ransom has spoken of the "search for the Unknown God" as an attribute of "many recent and living poets."[9] Titles among his books might suggest that he himself has found his God. But *God Without Thunder* is "an *unorthodox* defense of orthodoxy," a defense conducted not in terms of revelation, but of the signs of a healthy culture. And *Poems About God*, his first book, is not about one God but many Gods, as many Gods as there are human points of view; they are, taken together, a testimony to the ultimate Unknowableness of the One, a testimony that goes along with the preference in *God Without Thunder* for the mysterious God of the Old Testament to the cooperative, as Ransom describes Him, God of the New. However, in his mature poems, as in the novels of Forster, it is not a *search* for the Unknown God that is made so much as a rather shy and tentative gesture; "Somewhere Is Such a Kingdom" and "Persistent Explorer" make the same tentative signs as *Howards End* makes in the direction of what Forster calls the Unseen. They are the signs, incidentally, that identify Robert Frost as

8. A resemblance between them was pointed out by Isabel Gamble, "Ceremonies of Bravery: John Crowe Ransom," *Hopkins Review*, VI (Spring-Summer, 1953), 105–115.

9. Introduction, *Selected Poems of Thomas Hardy* (New York: Macmillan, 1961), p. xxxii.

a modern: "There may be little or much beyond the grave, / But the strong are saying nothing until they see" ("The Strong Are Saying Nothing").

Ransom and Forster are kinsmen also in their attitudes toward their arts: in their not supposing their purpose to be self-expression; in their acceptance of the limits of language, which is an indication, as Trilling says, of an acceptance of the human creature as he is. They are both "polite conversationalists." The term is one Ransom uses of Marvell—with whom he himself has been compared—in maintaining that the metaphysical effect need not depend upon wit or upon the extended conceit. "It is an effect possible to poets who are weighty yet idiomatic; polite conversationalists, perhaps, who do not have to make speeches in order to offer important observations."[10] Our poetic age, we have been reminded, is neo-Wordsworthian: our poets have gone back to actual speech. But whose speech? With Ransom it is that of the Gentleman, rather than that of the Common Man. The Gentleman is of no definite society usually—from the first the poet was determined not to "lapse" into "those amiable Southern accents"[11]—but of the Anglo-American culture. His sentences have the effect of an ease that can indulge itself in the direction of elegance, except in a few late poems, where they become more nervously elliptical, more conventionally modern. He is learned enough and assured enough to range in his words from the colloquial to the archaic or pedantic (the latter kinds in a tone frequently of self-mockery, for he is conscious of being human, all too human, and does not want his judgments to be taken as final). Or to play a Latinate vocabulary off against an Anglo-Saxon: "One of the forms that negative capability might take with a poet," Ransom has written, "would be this: to pass slyly back and forth between his two languages, if he is an English poet; as if he could not be expected to arrive at systematic theology with such a variable instrument."[12] The

10. "Why Critics Don't Go Mad," *Poems and Essays* (New York: Vintage Books, 1955), p. 155.

11. Introduction, *Poems About God* (New York: Henry Holt, 1919), p. vi.

12. "On Shakespeare's Language," *Poems and Essays*, p. 134.

effects of Ransom's poetry are almost exclusively effects of language, and effects that are possible almost exclusively through language. Its irony is a subtle, and gentle, irony of tone, rather than an irony of startling juxtaposition such as we have in Eliot. Imagery is of minimum importance in Ransom, and his poetry may therefore disappoint the reader who takes one of his chief delights in the image. But it is possible, perhaps, to make too much even of image in poetry. (I mean *image* here in the restricted sense of *picture*—Eliot's crab at the end of a stick—as distinct from metaphor and simile, which are also effects and means developed best through language.) If it is the image we want more than anything else, we can get it best from the graphic artist. In one sense Ransom's poetry might be said to be of the "purest" kind: in its fidelity to its medium.

What difficulty is the reader likely to encounter who picks up Ransom for the first time? I base my answer on what seems the usual experience of the interested undergraduate, who in an age when poetry is read almost only in the university is the closest we may come to a Common Reader, and on mistakes a few critics have fallen into. Because of Ransom's quietly toned, frequently understated discourse, the reader first may find him "cold." (Again I think of Forster, whose treatment of death has been mistaken in the same way.) It is an old misreading of Ransom, and not at all peculiar to the inexperienced reader: a young Southern poet and novelist has told me that he finds Ransom utterly heartless. So Ransom prefaced *Chills and Fever* with a kind of *caveat emptor,* "Agitato Ma Non Troppo," and he has written a slightly exasperated new beginning for it in *Selected Poems*:

> This is what the man said,
> Insisting, standing on his head.
>
> I have a grief,
> It was not stolen like a thief,
> Albeit I have no bittern by the lake
> To cry it up and down the brake.
>
> .   .   .   .   .   .

"Yes, there is grief in his mind,
But where is his fair child moaning in the wind?
Where is the white frost snowing on his head?
When did he stalk and weep and not loll in his bed?"

I will be brief,
Assuredly I know my grief,
And I am shaken; but not as a leaf.

Another error is due to a confusion of the genres that is endemic among modern readers. Because Ransom's poems are based often on a kind of narrative situation—that is, on the kind of situation that the prose fictionist could work with too—the reader may be led, as one generally admiring critic has been, to compare the poet to the novelists and come away complaining that his people are only types. Or he may be led to some extreme judgments, like another critic: to count "Here Lies a Lady," "Piazza Piece," "Hilda" and others as complete failures because the "characterizations" are flat, and to prefer a possibly inferior poem, like "Puncture," because it is a little more like a short story. George Pierce Baker ascribed the emphasis on characterization in modern drama (as opposed to the Elizabethan emphasis on plot) to the fact that modern theatergoers are trained less by seeing plays than by reading novels. The same may probably be said of most of us poetry readers. But the particularity of characterization we relish in the novel is not the kind available to lyric poetry generally, outside the dramatic monologue, and certainly not the kind that we have a right to demand of it. With many poems, in fact, we needlessly confuse ourselves by thinking in terms of character at all, especially when we mean the character of the "narrator," or "speaker," or "persona." The vagueness about the narrator of which the critic complains in "Here Lies a Lady" is due really to the fact that there is no narrator at all—that is, no speaker distinct from the poet, as long as we understand that by poet we do not mean the historical John Crowe Ransom. The *I* of "Here Lies a Lady" is no different from the *I* of "The Equilibrists," or "Spectral Lovers," or "Good Ships"; in these poems there is no intention to make the *I* a distinct character, with a distinct relation to other distinct characters, as the term "narrator" or "speaker" might imply.

To a third error the most sophisticated reader is liable. He may slip into it before he is aware, as into intellectual sin. Ransom is subtle in his irony, and the reader who has been trained by the modern critic to have sharp ears for irony, to be wary of taking almost anything at face value, may go too far and begin to imagine a whole complex of little ironies where none are intended. *Irony* is no doubt the most popular single term in our criticism, used not merely as a term of description, but as a term of almost unqualified praise: if the poem is ironic, we imply, the poem is successful. Ransom himself has commented on its over-emphasis.

Mr. Brooks is so insistent upon having in his poetry some irony, some form of "conflict" and "inclusion of opposites," that he has been led to make devastating slashes in the poetry of an English anthology that is now well shaken down and rather definitely accepted. . . . He seems to consider also that poetry has a specific, not in the hands of science, by which it can "resolve" or "reconcile" structural conflicts. My belief is that opposites can never be said to be resolved or reconciled merely because they have been got into the same poem, or got into the same complex of affective experience to create there a kind of "tension"; that if there is a resolution at all it must be a logical resolution; that when there is no resolution we have a poem without a structural unity; and that this is precisely the intention of irony, which therefore is something very special, and ought to be occasional.[13]

John Crowe Ransom is a very modest man, and he has had little to say about his own poems ("There's such a flashiness about the feel of your own composition,"[14] he has remarked.) But the accounts of the process of composition that he furnishes in *The World's Body* and *The New Criticism* would have to be relevant to his own practice. They apply, as he says, only

13. *The New Criticism*, pp. 94–95.
14. *Conversations* . . . , p. 30.

to the traditional poets, of whom he would of course make one, and not to the writers of free verse.

From passages in *The New Criticism* we can put together this condensed account of the poetic process.

The poem is an object comprising not two elements but four; not merely a meaning M, but D M, that part of a meaning which forms a logical structure, and I M, a part which does not belong to the structure and may be definitely illogical, though more probably it is only additive and a-logical; and not merely D S, a meter, but I S, a part of the total sound-effect which may be in exception to the law of the meter but at any rate does not belong to it.

.   .   .   .   .   .

But there are two kinds of indeterminacy in I M, and . . . the poet in metering his argument yields reluctantly to the first, as to an indeterminacy that means only inaccuracy and confusion, and then gladly to the second, as to an indeterminacy that opens to him a new world of discourse.

First, he tries to shift the language within the range of a rough verbal equivalence, and to alter D M no more substantively than necessary. A given word will probably have synonyms. The order of words in a phrase may be varied. A transitive predication may be changed to a passive; a relative clause to a participial phrase. In the little words denoting logical connections and transitions a good deal of liberty may be taken without being fatal; they may be expanded into something almost excessively explicit, or they may be even omitted, with the idea that the reader can supply the correct relations. A single noun may become a series of nouns, or nearly any other element may be compounded, without introducing much real novelty. Epithetical adjectives and adverbs may be interpolated, if they will qualify their nouns and verbs very obviously. Archaic locutions may be introduced for contemporary ones. A poet is necessarily an accomplished verbalist, and capable of an almost endless succession of periphrases that come nearer and nearer to metered language until finally he achieves what he wants; a language that is metrical enough, and close enough to his intended meaning.

.   .   .   .   .   .

But the important stage of indeterminacy comes, in the experiment of composition, when the imagination of the poet, and not only his verbal mechanics, is engaged. An "irrelevance" may feel forced at first, and its overplus of meaning unwanted, because it means the

importation of a little foreign or extraneous content into what should
be determinate, and limited; but soon the poet comes upon a kind
of irrelevance that seems desirable, and he begins to indulge it volun-
tarily, as a new and positive asset to the meaning. And this is the
principle: the importations which the imagination introduces into discourse have the value of developing the "particularity" which lurks
in the "body," and under the surface, of apparently determinate situations. When Marvell is persuaded by the rhyme-considerations to
invest the Humber with a tide, or to furnish his abstract calendar
with specifications about the Flood, and the conversion of the Jews,
he does not make these additions reluctantly. On the contrary, he
knows that the brilliance of the poetry depends on the shock, accom-
panied at once by the realism or the naturalism, of its powerful
particularity.[15]

Does this second kind of indeterminacy sound like mere
decoration? It is what previously he has called "texture of
meaning":

The relation of the meter to the meaning is that of a texture to
a structure. . . . But the finished poem will have even more important
texture than the phonetic. It will have texture of meaning too. . . . In
trying to find for the logical detail a substitute that will suit the
meter, the poet will discover presently that the best way is to explore
this detail to see what it contains, and to come up with facts which
belong to the detail but not to the logical structure; so a texture
of meaning is established with respect to the structure; and nothing
in poetry is so remarkable as this. It is the thing that peculiarly
qualifies a discourse as being poetic; it is its differentia.[16]

However:

It is not telling the whole truth to say that Shakespeare and other
accomplished poets resort to their variations, which are metrical im-
perfections, because a determinate meaning has forced them into it.
The poet likes the variations regardless of the meanings, finding them
essential in the capacity of a sound-texture to go with the sound-struc-
ture. It is in no very late stage of a poet's advancement that his
taste rejects a sustained phonetic regularity as something restricted
and barren, perhaps ontologically defective. Accordingly he is capable
of writing smooth meters and then roughening them on purpose. And
it must be added, while we are about it, that he is capable of writing

15. Pp. 301, 303–304, 314.
16. *Ibid.*, pp. 219–220.

a clean logical argument, and then of roughening that too, by introducing logical violence into it, and perhaps willful obscurity. We have
therefore this unusual degree of complexity in the total structure:
the indeterminate sound or the indeterminate meaning, I S or I M,
may have been really come to independently, by a poet who senses
the aesthetic value of indeterminateness and is veteran enough to go
straight after it. But nothing can be introduced into the meaning
without affecting the meter, and vice versa; so that I M, and not
only D M, . . . undetermines the meter again and produces I S; and,
conversely, I S, and not only D S, may un-determine the meaning
again and produce I M. It will sound very complicated, but good
poets will attest it all if we ask them.[17]

Although he speaks of the modern free verse writer's commitment "on principle to an unprecedented degree of indeterminateness in the meaning,"[18] his account of the traditional poet's composition allows for a good deal of "disrespect" to meaning—to
whatever meaning the poet may be conscious of at the beginning; it may have its chief value, in fact, merely in providing
a beginning.

Total intention is the total meaning of the finished poem, which differs
from the original logical content by having acquired a detail which
is immaterial to this content, being everywhere specific, or local, or
particular, and at any rate unpredictable. And what, precisely, is
the poet's intention at the beginning? It is to write a poem, and
that is, since he has written poems before, to turn his logical content
loose to shift for itself in the world of fortuitous experience; to get
out of the world of pure logical content. It is a disrespect to the
logic, if you are tremendously interested in the logic. If the given
logical content is a moral one, it is a disrespect to morality, if you
are devoted to that. It is a disrespect to morality in the degree that
it is a respect to something called "poetic" experience. Poetic experience is only to be had by disrespecting whatever kind of logical content we start with.[19]

This definition of the poetic experience is the basis of his call
for an "ontological critic," a critic who will not devote most
of his care to the exposition of what, to begin with, is better
provided for in other forms of discourse; of a poet's ideas, "a

17. *Ibid.*, pp. 324–325.
18. *Ibid.*, p. 334.
19. *Ibid.*, p. 224.

better version is almost certain to be found elsewhere in prose, so that their discussion under the poem is likely to be a tame affair."[20] This probably is the point of his critical theory that has had the largest influence.

The most important stage of composition to Ransom is the revision. The skillful poet is surer of his second thoughts than of his first; "second thoughts tend to be the richer, for in order to get them he has to break up the obvious trains of association and explore more widely."[21] He is insistent upon the indispensability of meter in the process.

The first version of the poem that comes out just drives us wild—we *know* we've got a poem there, but it's like an untamed tiger; we haven't got him firmly. We haven't got him by the right place and we must do something about it—we must revise the poem. There's no way to revise a poem—and some young poets are without the capacity to do this which would indicate that they lack something of the gift of being a poet—without taking the very same situation, shutting our eyes, and submitting it again to the imagination to see what's there: To see if better little aspects, little angles, of that experience won't turn up. Well now, it's hopeless if you go out into the woods, say, and say well, I'll rewrite this poem. You sit down and ponder but the thing won't come back, and you don't know what you're looking for, really. But now suppose there are places where the meter is unsatisfactory—and there always are—the meter's too rough. Or sometimes it's too smooth and it's got to be roughened up in order to get that counterpoint. And so we're looking at it with a metrical consideration: Here are two words coming together which mustn't come together; here is a phrase of four words which doesn't make any meter at all—and the prose is so powerful in it that nothing would disturb it. And so we then think of verbal changes—and then verbal suggestions come in; or we think of rhymes and then we can easily figure on other rhymes. And we may be sure that after we have tinkered with a poem to improve or perfect or establish its meters, that the thing we finally pick as our poem will not be merely metrically acceptable, but it will have powerful imaginative quality. We are looking at it from all angles, though our attention is concentrated on finding the metrical feature.[22]

He himself has declined to write free verse since *Poems About God*.

20. *Ibid.,* p. 302.
21. *The World's Body* (New York: Charles Scribner's Sons, 1938), p. 11.
22. *Conversations* . . . , pp. 24–25.

And he is insistent upon anonymity as "a condition of poetry." To the degree that the writer fails to abandon his "prose self" for "an ideal or fictitious personality," his composition fails of being poetry:

Poets may go to universities and, if they take to education, increase greatly the stock of ideal selves into which they may pass for the purpose of being poetical. If on the other hand they insist too narrowly on their own identity and their own story, inspired by a simple but mistaken theory of art, they find their little poetic fountains drying up within them. Milton set out to write a poem mourning a friend and poet who had died; in order to do it he became a Greek shepherd, mourning another one. It was not that authority attached particularly to the discourse of a Greek shepherd; the Greek shepherd in his own person would have been hopeless; but Milton as a Greek shepherd was delivered from being Milton the scrivener's son, the Master of Arts from Cambridge, the handsome and finicky young man, and that was the point. . . . Today young men and women, as noble as Milton, those in university circles as much as those out of them, try to become poets on another plan, and with rather less success. They write their autobiographies, following perhaps the example of Wordsworth, which on the whole may have been unfortunate for the prosperity of the art; or they write some of their intenser experiences, their loves, pities, griefs, and religious ecstacies; but too literally, faithfully, piously, ingenuously. They seem to want to do without wit and playfulness, dramatic sense, detachment, and it cuts them off from the practice of an art.[23]

Merrill Moore, Fugitive and later psychiatrist, once remarked to Ransom, "I think that I could collect a Ransom Omnibus that would be more objective, or more representative, of the real man than your *Selected Poems*."[24] That, to Ransom, would be beside the point. The point is art, and the point of art is not self-expression.

Ransom wrote most of his poetry between 1916—he began at the comparatively late age of twenty-eight—and 1927, a period made even briefer by the interruption of World War I (he

23. *The World's Body*, pp. 2–3.
24. *Fugitives' Reunion: Conversations at Vanderbilt, May 3–5, 1956*, ed. Rob Roy Purdy (Nashville: Vanderbilt University Press, 1959), p. 147.

was in France when his first volume came out). He did not undergo a gradual development of theme or of style. His mature themes are already in *Poems About God,* and his mature style he came into overnight, as it seemed to Tate, sometime in the winter of 1921–22. He exhibits still a third style in the seven pieces in *Selected Poems* that he wrote at intervals between 1927 and 1963.

Why has he not written more poetry? He says that he has "nothing to reply" to that question. "My talent was a modest one, and I did the best I could. . . . I don't like to be held to any concept of magnitude or dimension. And every poet is a law to himself in those matters."[25] Two notions often met are that criticism is the refuge of poets who have run dry, or that it is what causes them to go dry to begin with. Ransom says simply, "I never tried to write and found I couldn't. I just got involved in some of these theoretical questions—philosophical questions—and they just engage my whole mind."[26] But Tate was probably right when he suggested in his review of *Two Gentlemen in Bonds*—inferior he thought to *Chills and Fever*—that another book might be redundant. It is in keeping with the character of Ransom, as other Fugitives have described it and as we sense it in his writings, that he has not thought of his poetry in the nervous terms of a career to be furthered, that he has not joined in the present-day Cult of the Professional.

Since Ransom's volume is small and his themes rather few in number, my procedure in the following pages is the simple one of considering some of the best poems one by one, few of which have received close readings. Although I take them up in a loosely chronological order, I use the latest text, that of the 1963 *Selected Poems.* Ransom has been a tireless and in most cases inspired reviser, though in others he may seem merely fussy. An appendix shows the changes he has made over the years in some of his most important poems.

25. *Fugitives' Reunion*, p. 81.
26. *Conversations* . . . , p. 30.

| Chapter II | *Poems About God* |

As Randall Jarrell remarked, Ransom's thorough winnowing of his poems has made much of the criticism that might have been written unnecessary. Into his *Selected Poems* Ransom has allowed none of his *Poems About God,* and no one has complained, as some complained about other exclusions from the 1945 *Selected Poems,* that Ransom has been too hard on his early work. Since he himself has allowed these poems to die quietly, it would be pointless to belabor their awkwardness or their flatness, or the appearance of haste they give when set beside the later poems. But we *are* curious about the apprentice work of our writers, and I would like to give a sample of Ransom's, which has long been out of print. In it are some of Ransom's later themes—especially his major theme, mortality—but more directly treated, the direct treatment evidence that Ransom's characteristic control was hard-won and is not the constitutional fastidiousness that it has been mistaken for.

Ransom began to write poetry while an instructor at Vanderbilt in 1916. "One day of days I remember well," Donald Davidson recalls.

My teacher, John Ransom, beckoned me aside and led me to a shady spot on the campus near the streetcar stop called "Vanderbilt Stile"— though the stile had long since yielded to an open entrance. Ransom drew a sheet of paper from his pocket. Almost blushingly, he announced that he had written a poem. It was his very first, he said. He wanted to read it to me. He read it, and I listened—admiringly, you may be sure. The title of the poem was "Sunset." But in that moment, I suppose, was the actual dawn of the "Fugitive movement."[1]

In the poem a young man addresses his lady as they watch the sun set on the meadows and fields.

> I know you are not cruel,
> And you would not willingly hurt anything in the world.
>
> . . . . . .
>
> I thought you would some day begin to love me,
> But now I doubt it badly;
> It is no man-rival I am afraid of,
> It is God.
>
> The meadows are very wide and green,
> And the big field of wheat is solid gold,
> Or a little darker than gold.
>
> . . . . . .
>
> But to you
> It is God.
>
> . . . . . .
>
> Your eyes are not regarding me,
> Nor the four-leaf clovers I picked for you,
> (With a prayer and a gentle squeeze for each of them),
> Nor are they fretting over dress, and shoes,
> And image in the little glass,
> Restlessly,
> Like the eyes of other girls.
> You are looking away over yonder
> To where the crooked rail-fence gets to the top
> Of the yellow hill
> And drops out of sight
> Into space.
> Is that infinity that catches it?
> And do you catch it too in your thoughts?
> I know that look;
> I have not seen it on another girl;
> And it terrifies me,
> For I cannot tell what it means,
> But I think
> It has something to do with God.

1. *Southern Writers in the Modern World* (Athens: University of Georgia Press, 1958), p. 14.

Each of the five verse-paragraphs ends with the word *God*.

Ransom's "earliest intellectual recollection," according to John
L. Stewart, "was of a fury against abstraction."[2] There is abstraction which is *extraction*—the sense in which Ransom uses
the word in *God Without Thunder* to designate the method of
scientific discourse—and there is abstraction which is idealiza-
tion, the way of the girl in the poem, for whom the details of
the scene have value only as means by which to approach the
Absolute; even the cows, in her "strange eyes," share in a universal movement "towards the sunset." But the mellow glow
of the girl's idealizing obscures the landscape's features, and his
own, in a way the young man finds deadly. The way of the
living is to relish the infinity of the finite, the immeasurable
uniqueness of scene and moment:

> Two people never sat like us by a fence of cedar rails
> On a still evening
> And looked at such fat fields.

For the smallest object is infinite, in the sense that it is unique.

The pebble is too stubborn for the geometer: it is an infinite. However
minutely or microscopically he may study the parts of its surface,
he will find no law, no type, no denominator by which their values
are all commensurable. His determinate or ideal reductions are much
too simple.[3]

As for idealists, Ransom in one of his stronger statements has
written:

Persons who are idealists by conviction, or on general principles, are
simply monsters. (I mean the Platonic ones, the kind of idealists
who worship universals, laws, Platonic ideas, reason, the "immaterial.") Unlike the scientists, they are of no use, yet they wilfully
take upon themselves the disability of the scientists, and not only
do they have no pleasure in individual objects but they even solicit
the public to make the same sacrifice. Professionally they tend to
be philosophers, preachers, and educators, and from these positions

2. *John Crowe Ransom* (Minneapolis: University of Minnesota Press, 1962),
p. 9.

3. Ransom, *God Without Thunder*, p. 281.

infect us with their vice and keep us, in the range of our interest, more like animals and less like human beings than we have a right to be.

I do not think the term vice is too strong.[4]

But the young man is too gallant to call his lady a monster. Mild, long-suffering, and self-mocking—

> I am stirred,
> I say grand and wonderful, and grow adjectival—

he is little different from the typical speaker of the later poems. Nor is he the last frustrated lover that we will meet. The poem is, however, Ransom's only published experiment in free verse.

When shortly he had written enough poems for a book, Christopher Morley, who had been a friend at Oxford and had published some of the poems in his columns in New York and Philadelphia newspapers, helped him find a publisher. Also involved was Robert Frost (to whom some reviewers of the book were to compare Ransom):

> There was a year when I lost, sort of, my job and I hadn't anything and there was a lull in everything, selling books, around that time and Holt's gave me a hundred dollars a month to live on with the understanding that I'd read any manuscript they sent me. They only sent me two manuscripts for the year—and one was his *Poems* about God, and the other I won't mention.
>
> But John was sort of my discovery. They printed him. John has repudiated those first poems I believe; he doesn't think so much of them. . . .
>
> But he had the art, and he had the tune.[5]

In his introduction to his first book, the poet, "John Crowe Ransom, 1st Lieut. Field Artillery, A.E.F.," is not only remarkably, though understandably, detached, but also seems a little dissatisfied already with his poems, hinting of a future suppression.

---

4. *The World's Body*, p. 225.

5. Frost, *Conversations* . . . , pp. 11–12. "In 1952 Frost told a group at Dartmouth College that Ransom was his favorite among living American poets" (Stewart, *The Burden of Time: The Fugitives and Agrarians* [Princeton, N.J.: Princeton University Press, 1965], p. 250).

Most of these poems about God were complete a year ago, that is at about the time when the great upheaval going on in God's world engulfed our country too. Since then I have added a little only, and my experience has led me so wide that I can actually look back upon those antebellum accomplishments with the eye of the impartial spectator, or at most with a fatherly tenderness, no more. In this reviewing act I find myself thinking sometimes that the case about God may not be quite so desperate as the young poet chooses to believe. But it is not for that reason that I shall ever think of suppressing a single one of his poems. For I am deeply engaged by the downright evident honesty of the young man, though I may wonder at the source of his excitement; esteeming honesty more highly than those amiable Southern accents into which he seems determined not to lapse, and indeed more highly than anything else in the world.

He goes on to explain the plan of the book:

The first three or four poems that I ever wrote (that was two years ago) were done in three or four different moods and with no systematic design. I was therefore duly surprised to notice that each of them made considerable use of the term God. I studied the matter a little, and came to the conclusion that this was the most poetic of all terms possible; was a term always being called into requisition during the great moments of the soul, now in tones of love, and now indignantly; and was the very last word that a man might say when standing in the presence of that ultimate mystery to which all our great experiences reduce.

Wishing to make my poems as poetic as possible, I simply likened myself to a diligent apprentice and went to work to treat rather systematically a number of the occasions on which this term was in use with common American men. . . . I very quickly ruled that I should consider only those situations as suitable in which I could imagine myself pronouncing the name God sincerely and spontaneously, never by that way of routine which is death to the aesthetic and religious emotions.

I anticipate the objection that the name of God is frequently taken here in ways that are not the ways of the fathers. I reply in advance, There are many mountains; and probably every one of them is worthy of being charted on the true Chart of God's world.[6]

His detached tone is matched in a little story told about him by Robert Penn Warren:

6. Pp. v-vii.

I encountered in California some years ago a man named McClure, who edits the paper at Santa Monica. . . . He was in France at the same time that John was as a soldier. . . . And he said that he was walking down the street with John Ransom, who was a good soldierly companion of his during that period, and they went to get the mail at the battery mail distribution. And they got a few letters, and John got a little package. And he opened the little package, and there were two copies of *Poems About God* in it. And he said John hadn't seen the book before, and he opened it and inspected it with composure, and then turned to McClure and said, "I'd like to give you a copy of this."[7]

However, the book impressed Robert Graves when it "strayed to Oxford in the pocket of a Southern Rhodes scholar" around 1921. "I could not rest until I had, with Ransom's approval, edited a selection from both *Poems About God* and [*Chills and Fever*] and arranged that it got proper recognition in the English press."[8] Graves's edition, published in 1924 as *Grace After Meat,* includes nine of the thirty-three pieces in *Poems About God.*

Not every poem in *Poems About God* mentions God directly; but of those that do not, most approach that ultimate term, as in the statement of the conflict between body and soul in "The Swimmer." Worn down by the "dog-days," when "grasses on the upland broil" and "eggs and meats and Christians spoil," the swimmer would resolve the conflict in favor of soul, whose voice is the voice of reason, and let himself sink to the bottom of the water.

> What do I need of senses five?
> Why eat, or drink, or sweat, or wive?
> What do we strive for when we strive?
> What do we live for when we live?
> And what if I do not rise again,
> Never to goad a heated brain
> To hotter excesses of joy and pain?
> Why should it be against the grain
> To lie so cold and still and sane?

The water represents infinity to the swimmer, washing his body

7. *Fugitives' Reunion,* pp. 101–102.
8. Graves, "Muscular Poetry," *The Saturday Review of Literature,* Dec. 27, 1924, p. 412.

> The color of leaves in a starlight scene,
> . . . as white as the stars between.

It is the soul's "native seat" and "forgiving element," "so long by forfeiture escheat." (*Escheat* anticipates the diction of the mature poems.) "The garden's curse is at last unsaid." But man is meant to find no such easy resolution of his dualistic state. To man, in Ransom's view, good itself is meaningless without evil. Whether the swimmer go through with a literal suicide or not, he is the "wicked swimmer" for having, in the langauge of the later "Painted Head," "traduced the flesh."

> Water-bugs play shimmer-shimmer,
> Naked body's just a glimmer,
> Watch ticks every second grimmer:
> *Come to the top, O wicked swimmer!*

The dualism of body and soul is approached from the opposite angle in "The Cloak Model." A stranger, "a dismal daffy one," calls a young man aside to look at a store-window mannequin.

> "Observe how ripe the lady's lips,
> How Titianesque the mop of hair,
> And where the great white shoulder dips
> Beneath its gauzy half-eclipse,
> You may well stare and stare.
>
> "When I was young I said as you
> Are saying in your sapphic youth,
> That ah! such lips were certain cue,
> And look! her bosom's rhythm too,
> It signified her truth;
>
> "Her broad brow meant intelligence
> And something better than a bone,
> Her body's curves were spirit's tents,
> Her fresh young skin was innocence
> Instead of meat that shone.
>
> "I wish the moralists would thresh
> (Indeed the thing is very droll)
> God's oldest joke, forever fresh:
> The fact that in the finest flesh
> There isn't any soul."

The stanza Ransom used in "The Cloak Model" he used again later, with a little variation in the rhyme scheme, in "Philomela," "Eclogue," and "Puncture": five lines with two rhyme sounds, the fifth line short. The short last line is a favorite device of his, to underline an irony or to understate.

There are other early examples of the war of opposites that informs Ransom's verse. In "A Christmas Colloquy" the opposites are represented by a poor preacher and his seven-year-old daughter, "misunderstanding one another." Its motto might be Sir Toby Belch's "Dost thou think, because thou art virtuous, there shall be no more cakes and ale?"

> ANN:
> Father, what will there be for me
> To-morrow on the Christmas tree?
> Have you told Santa what to bring,
> My pony, my doll, and everything?
>
> THOMAS:
> My daughter, Santa will know best
> What to bring you, and what the rest.
> But father and his little girl
> And everybody in the world
> Should dwell to-night on the higher things,
> For hark! the herald angel sings,
> And in a manger poor and lowly
> Lies little Jesus, high and holy.
>
> ANN:
> Father, don't talk of little Jesus,
> You're only doing it to tease us,
> It isn't nearly time for bed,
> And I want to know what Santa said.
>
> THOMAS:
> Jesus is better than any toys
> For little sinning girls and boys,
> For Jesus saves, but sin destroys.
> And O, It gives him sad surprise,
>
> There must be tears in Jesus' eyes,
> When little girls with bad behavior
> Forget to own their Lord and Savior.

ANN:
I didn't, you know it isn't true!
I say my prayers, I always do,
I know about Jesus very well,
And God the Father, Heaven, and Hell.
O please don't say it any more,
You've said it so many times before,
But tell me all about Santa instead,
And about the horns on his reindeer's head,
And what he will bring me on his sled.

THOMAS:
This night he was born on earth for us,
And can my daughter mock him thus,
And care more for her worldly pleasures
Than Jesus' love and heavenly treasures?
For Jesus didn't like to be
So crowned with thorns and nailed to tree,
But there was a sinful world to free,
And out he went to Gethsemane—

ANN:
And left the twelve and went apart—
O father, I know it off by heart,
Please, father, please don't finish it out,
There's so much else to talk about!
I ask about Santa, and there you go,
And now you're spoiling my Christmas so,
And you are the wickedest man I know!

Finally Ann is sent to bed crying. The scene meanwhile has disturbed the old setter by the fire.

Inez, who had been perplexed
To see good kinsfolk so much vexed,
When peace descended on the twain,
Lay down beside the fire again.

As in the later "Necrological," Ransom uses the simplicity of the animal to set off the human dilemma of living in contradictory worlds. To be a man of God and to be a father are in this instance opposing duties. That, E. M. Forster would say,— and it is Ransom's unspoken imperative as well—is when one must let proportion come in.

The speaker in "Friendship" makes a universal mistake:

> I viewed him well, the visible fat fool,
> And yet I took him in; for I contended,
> Friends are not sent in order of our choosing,
> They come unsuited like the gifts of God.
> I would not do a perfidy to friendship,
> I let him past the private inner gate.

Now his friend "forages at will" upon his "garden," "noses all its pretty secrets out," without finding anything he approves.

> Meeting a modest velveteen affair,
> Peevish he hangs his sad and silly head:
> "Alas! such unsubstantial gaudy goods!"
>
> .   .   .   .   .
>
> And not a perfume spills upon the air
> But his malicious nose suspects a poison,
> As he goes browsing like an ancient ass,
> An old distempered ass.
>
> .   .   .   .   .
>
> "O friend, is this the harvest of your hands?
> How will you stand before the lord of harvests?
> These are the gardens of your idleness;
> Where is the vineyard, friend?"

The opposition between the aesthetic and the practical is met also in "One Who Rejected Christ," about the champion farmer contemptuous of his neighbors for leaving the ground by their fences for rose bushes.

> seeing that roses yield no rent
> I cut the stuff away.
>
> .   .   .   .   .
>
> For crops are all that a good field grows,
> And nothing is worse than a sniff of rose
> In the good strong smell of hay.

But the sense of the title "The Christian" seems to be a somewhat derogatory equation of Christianity with the feminine principle, as in Nietzsche. The title is given to a poem about

"a surly sort of mariner" who married and settled down in "a
precious little house," where

> he weathered many winter seasons,
> Knocking the ashes neatly from his pipe
> Upon the tended hearth.

> And only when he went upon the moors,
> And felt the sting and censure of the winds,
> And tasted of the salt blown in from sea,
> Then only would he curse the marriage morning,
> And swear he'd not go skulking back again
> To sit that hearth like any broken bitch
> Whose running time was over.

There is the final duality of Manicheism in the view of God
given in "Prayer" and "Sickness." In the former an old woman
labors to church on a hot Sunday to "abuse her superannuate
knees" in prayer for an erring son; God is not deaf to her prayers
but simply limited, like the best intentioned ruler, in His power
to spare His subjects the ills of the world. The tone is light,
the tone of the last verse-paragraph especially resembling the
tones with which Ransom would later approach the serious:

> Now God sat beaming on his burnished throne
> And swept creation with appraising eye,
> Finding, I fear, not all was free from blemish,
> Yet keeping his magnificent composure;
> But wearing certain necessary airs,
> To suit with such incumbency of court,
> He still at heart was quite a gentleman;
> For when he saw that aged lady drooping
> And wearying her bones with genuflections
> For her unworthiness, he fell ashamed
> To think how hard it went with holy women
> To ease their poor predicaments by prayer:
> There on his heaven, and heard of all the hosts,
> He groaned, he made a mighty face so wry
> That several seraphin forgot their harping
> And scolded thus: "O what a wicked woman,
> To shrew his splendid features out of shape!"

In "Sickness" God is a pitying but helpless watcher at the death-
bed of "the toughest carcass in the town."

"Now, Lord, I die: is there no word,
No countervail that God can say?"
No word. But tight upon his arm,
Was God, and drew not once away
Until his punctual destiny.
To whom could God repair to pray?

As Ransom's introduction promises, there are a number of ways in which the name of God is taken. In "Geometry" He is "a crazy God," man being the source of order in the world.

My window looks upon a wood
That stands as tangled as it stood
When God was centuries too young
To care how right he worked, or wrong,
His patterns in obedient trees,
Unprofited by the centuries
He still plants on as crazily
As in his drivelling infancy.

. . . . . .

An easy thing to improve on God,
Simply the knowing of even from odd,
Simply to count and then dispose
In patterns everybody knows,
Simply to follow curve and line
In geometrical design.

Gardeners only cut their trees
For nobler regularities.
But from my window I have seen
The noblest patch of quivering green
Lashed till it never quivered again.
God had a fit of temper then,
And spat shrill wind and lightning out
At twinges of some godly gout.
But as for me, I keep indoors
Whenever he starts his awful roars.
What can one hope of a crazy God
But lashings from an aimless rod?

It is the way God presents Himself in Hardy's "New Year's Eve":

"Sense-sealed I have wrought, without a guess
That I evolved a consciousness
        To ask for reasons why.

"Strange that ephemeral creatures who
        By my own ordering are,
Should see the shortness of my view,
Use ethic tests I never knew,
        Or made provision for!"

He sank to raptness as of yore,
        And opening New Year's Day
Wove it by rote as theretofore,
And went on working evermore
        In his unweeting way.

The theme of God's "aimless rod" receives more somber treatment in "Grace," a narrative of 116 lines which Graves had
to persuade Ransom to let him reprint in *Grace After Meat,*
Ransom having come to dislike the poem "on the grounds of
its hastiness and ugliness."[9] It is about a pious but otherwise
anonymous hired man—he is given no name—who shows up
frequently at the narrator's gate early in the morning,

Saying he thought he'd help me work
That field of corn before the rain;
And I never spoke of the dollar a day,
It's no use causing hired men pain,
But slipped it into his hand at dark
While he undid the coupling chain;
And whistled a gospel tune, and knew
He'd join in strong on the refrain.
For I would pitch the treble high,
"Down at the cross where my Savior died,"
And then he rolled along the bass,
"There did I bury my sin and pride."

Sinful pride of a hired man!
Out of a hired woman born!

One hot day the hired man looks worn from the morning's plow-
ing. The narrator takes him to the house for dinner, and after-

9. Graves, Introduction, *Grace After Meat* (London: Hogarth Press, 1924), p. 8.

ward they rest in the shade awhile; but when they return to
the field, the sun is still bearing down.

I hoped we'd get a bit of breeze
And thought the hired man was used
To God's most blazing cruelties.

Sundays, the hired man would pray
To live in the sunshine of his face;
Now here was answer come complete,
Rather an overdose of grace!

He fell in the furrow, an honest place
And an easy place for a man to fall.
His horse went marching blindly on
In a beautiful dream of a great fat stall.
And God shone on in merry mood,
For it was a foolish kind of sprawl,
And I found a hulk of heaving meat
That wouldn't answer me at all.

. . . . . .

I caught him up with all my strength
And with a silly stumbling tread
I dragged him over the soft brown dirt
And dumped him down beside the shed.

I thought of the prayers the fool had prayed
To his God, and I was seeing red,
When all of a sudden he gave a heave
And then with shuddering—vomited!
And God, who had just received full thanks
For all his kindly daily bread,
Now called it back again—perhaps
To see that his birds of the air were fed.
Not mother's dainty dinner now,
A rather horrible mess instead,
Yet all of it God required of him
Before the fool was duly dead.

Even of deaths there is a choice,
I've seen you give a good one, God,
But he in his vomit laid him down,
Denied the decency of blood.

God's name is invoked in happier moments. The mindlessly cruel Nature of "Geometry" and "Grace" becomes, to the admirer of one of her scenes in "By the Riverside," the best of all possible worlds:

> The sinner's mocking tongue is dry,
> Wonder is on that mighty jeerer,
> He loves, and he never loved before,
> He wants the glowing sky no nearer,
> He likes the willows to be two,
> He would not have the water clearer,
> He thinks that God is perfect once:
> Heaven, rejoice! a new God-fearer.

God is worshipped in the kitchen by a farm boy in "Noonday Grace" (the one poem in the book that seems entirely amateurish, like the verse that people submit to their local newspapers):

> He's infinite, and all of that,
> The setting sun his habitat,

but "his greatest joy" is "to have big dinners for his boy."

> In fact, he helps my mother cook,
> And slips to the dining-room door to look;
> And when we are at our noon-day meal,
> He laughs to think how fine we feel.
>
> An extra fork is by my plate,
> I nearly noticed it too late!
>
> Mother, you're keeping a secret back!
> I see the pie-pan through the crack,
> Incrusted thick in gold and black.
>
> There's no telling what that secret pair
> Have cooked for me in the kitchen there,
>
> There's no telling what that pie can be,
> But tell me that it's blackberry!
>
> As long as I keep topside the sod,
> I'll love you always, mother and God.

Or in "Worship,"

> God is sweetest of all
> Discovered in a drinking hall.
>
> For God requires no costly wine
> But comes on the foam of a crockery stein.
>
> And when that foam is on the lips,
> Begin then God's good fellowships.

In the gymnasium of "Dumb-Bells,"

> Thirty fat men of the town
> Must sweat their filthy paunches down.
> Dripping sweat and pumping blood
> They try to make themselves like God.

In "Wrestling," one of the book's better poems, God's name seems to figure at first only as an interjection. The setting of the poem is "threshing-time, the manly season."

> We kept the thresher thundering by daylight,
> And rested all the sweeter after dark,
> Telling of tales, and washing in the river.

One of the hands, "some twenty miles a stranger," boasts that he has never lost a wrestling match.

> We had a champion there. He looked and listened,
> He measured off his man, he made his mind up,
> And thus he brought great honor to his county:
> "My friend, I've heard you bragging, heard you braying,
> And now I say, for God's sake come and wrestle."
> And thus appealed, the other came, for God's sake,
> And they did wrestle.

By the end of the poem the effect of the name is more than that of mere exclamation; the "by God" of the final verse paragraph, spoken by a voice at first mysterious, suggests that it is only "by God"—by God's favor—that the county champion is able to triumph:

But while the tide of battle ran so equal,
I heard a sound, I took it for a voice,
I almost saw it, spitting out a passage
Between the haggard jaws of my poor hero,
The voice as of a man almost despairing,
Hoping again though all his hopes had failed:
"By God, I'll have you down in one more minute!"
And it was as he said; for in a minute
He had him down, by God.

A poem about two strong men turns out to be a poem about the limits of man's strength. The lines which describe the wrestlers' furthest exertions,

They sprang, they gripped, they strained and rocked and
    twisted,
They pounded much good sod to dust and powder,

are touched with irony in the verbs; these are not the words of an aficionado, absorbed in the strength and grace of the athletes—no holds are described, no half-nelsons or headlocks—but the words of a somewhat detached spectator who cannot entirely shake a sense of human puniness, even here, and who might be imagined recalling, as he watches them pound "much good sod to dust," what the Bible says will come of human flesh. These lines, of course, do not set the tone of the whole poem: the poem ends with a victory; but they allude to the context of human victories, a context that Ransom would say makes them seem all the sweeter, as the labor of the threshers by daylight makes their rest "all the sweeter after dark."

Mortality is the theme of two other of the book's better pieces. The quatrains of "Under the Locusts" tell us what the old men are saying as they sit in the shade:

Dick's a sturdy little lad
Yonder throwing stones;
Agues and rheumatic pains
Will fiddle on his bones.

Grinny Bob is out again
Begging for a dime;
Niggers haven't any souls,
Grinning all the time.

> Jenny and Will go arm in arm.
> He's a lucky fellow;
> Jenny's cheeks are pink as rose,
> Her mother's cheeks are yellow.
>
> War is on, the paper says,
> Wounds and enemies;
> Now young gallivanting bucks
> Will know what trouble is.
>
> Parson's coming up the hill,
> Meaning mighty well;
> Thinks he's preached the doubters down.
> And old men never tell.

In "The Resurrection," the only example in *Poems About God* of the sonnet form with which Ransom would later have a good deal of success, the old men are met along the highway,

> Their stoic backs as plain as graveyard stones,
> An epitaph of poor dead men indeed.
>
> .   .   .   .   .   .
>
> "What pretty piece of hope then have you spun,
> My old defeated traveler," I say,
> "That keeps you marching on? For I have none.
> I have looked often and I have not found
> Old men bowed low who ever rose up sound."

These poems are less metaphorical than the later poems, but a happily conceived metaphor does form the basis of "Roses." The poem has nothing to do with God, though Ransom as in several other such poems kept faith with his central design by mechanically working His name in anyway: here in the phrase "God knows," which drags along an "I suppose."

> I entered dutiful, God knows,
> The room in which I was to sit
> With dreary unbelieving books.
> It was surprising, I suppose,
> To find such happy change in it.

The surprise he finds is "a most celestial rose" that "looked the flower that my love looks," who herself has placed it there. Then the man experiences a kind of epiphany.

I went like one escaping hell
To drink its fragrance and to touch,
And stroked, O ludicrous to tell!
A horrid thing of bric-a-brac,
A make-believe, a mockery,
And nothing that a rose should be.

Red real roses keep a thorn,
And save their loveliness a while
And in their perfect date unfold.
But you, beyond all women born,
Have spent so easily your smile,
That I am not the less forlorn
Nor these ironic walls less cold,
Because it smiles, the chilly rose,
As you are smiling, I suppose.

"November," the poem that follows in what we may assume
to be a deliberate pairing, treats with sympathy another lady
of easy favors, so that the standard by which the first lady is
measured would seem a more relative one than chastity. It is
a long poem, uneven, but fine in its evocation of mood.

There's a patch of trees at the edge of the field,
And a brown little house that is kept so warm,
And a woman waiting by the hearth
Who still keeps most of a woman's charm.

She traffics in her woman's goods
And is my woman of affairs.
Yet not so fast, my moral men,
November's most poetic airs
Are heavy with old lovers' tales,
How hearths are holy with their prayers,
How women give their fragrance up
And give their love to the man that dares.
Now who goes heedless hearing that?
At last we trade, we laissez-faires.

His mother has picked out a nice girl for him,

Who sings soprano in the choir
And swallows Christian doctrine straight.
Of all the girls deliver me
From the girl you haven't the heart to hate!

But his mind, as "the winds of late November droop" and pass about the farm, is still on a girl whom he courted years before.

> If God had heard my prayer then,
> The good folk couldn't point and say
> As mother says they're pointing now:
> Behold, one stands in the sinners' way!
> The stiffest sceptic bends his neck
> And stands on no more vain parley
> If such as she would have him come,
> Worship with her in the Baptist way,
> Accept the fables as he can,
> A Jewish God, a Passion Play;
> And such a lover never comes
> To fondling dirty drabs for pay.
> But God had another man for her,
> He cannot answer all that pray.
>
> November winds are weak and cold,
> They lie at last beneath the blue
> And sleep in the fields as cold as they.
> I know but one good thing to do.
>
> . . . . . .
>
> My woman waits by the hearth, I say,
> And what is a scarlet woman to you?
> Her sins are scarlet if you will,
> Her lips are hardly of that hue,
> And many a time I've seen her sit
> Beside the hearth an hour or two,
> And set the pot upon the fire
> And wait until she's spoken to.
> A hateful owl is roosting near
> Who mocks my woman, Hoo, Hoo, Hoo,
> But the pot sings back just as shrill as it can,
> And the angry fire-log crashes through;
> And there the woman waits, and I,
> I ponder the ways of God—and rue!

Another poem on the subject of love was praised by Graves—extravagantly, as it now seems to us—as the only poem to be compared with "Winter Remembered" in "Modern American

Poetry."[10] It seems to have been a favorite with Ransom's first readers; at the Fugitives' reunion Alfred Starr called "The Lover" the poem that "may live forever in this group."[11] The lover in the poem as yet loves secretly, not having overcome the new lover's pride ("Must I confess before the pack / Of babblers, idiots, and such?") and, perhaps, timidity; but he has the guilty man's urge to talk about the crime he cannot confess to, and so he has sat among friends and "wagged" his "wicked tongue" on love and women, pretending misogyny.

> And when your name was spoken too,
> I did not change, I did not start,
> And when they only praised and loved,
> I still could play my secret part,
> Cursing and lies upon my tongue,
> And songs and shouting in my heart.
>
> But when you came and looked at me,
> You tried my poor pretence too much.
> O love, do you know the secret now
> Of one who would not tell nor touch?
>
>   .   .   .   .   .   .
>
> O too much glory shut with us!
> O walls too narrow and opaque!
> O come into the night with me
> And let me speak, for Jesus' sake.

In "The School," the last poem that we will look at in the volume, love is one of the subjects at which the poet cocks his more ironic eye, along with money and intellect. The title refers really to two schools: the academy, and what to the irritation of schoolmasters is commonly named as the opposite to the academy, "the world." In the former, the young man in the poem is "equipped with Grecian thoughts"; therefore,

10. *The Saturday Review of Literature*, Dec. 27, 1924, p. 412. The capitals are Graves's and are for irony, Graves being somewhat condescending here and in his introduction to *Grace After Meat* toward American poetry and poetic taste.

11. *Fugitives' Reunion*, p. 80.

                          how could I live
Among my father's folk? My father's house
Was narrow and his fields were nauseous.
I kicked his clods for being common dirt,
Worthy a world which never could be Greek.

                    .   .   .   .   .   .

The Lord preserves his saints for Christian uses.
He sent a pair of providential eyes.
They would have sat in any witless head,
Although I deemed them deep as classic seas,
As strange as any woman written smiling,
And much more near; the merest modern eyes,
The first my Athens faced; and yet her lamp,
It flickered rather low.

Then he commanded me to scrutiny
As to a fingered thing of no great matter,
A circumstantial sorry little coin.
A friendly thing, I owned, to lie so warm
Against the side of any friendless man;
And in the hand—O if the happy hand
Accommodate the cunning rounded scepter,
Then is dominion seated in that palm,
And coveting is seated in men's eyes.
Make haste, my hands, about your own inclosures!

There is a complexity of attitude in "The School" that we do
not find in another of these early poems. In "A Christmas Colloquy," in "Friendship," the opposing attitudes are represented
by two opposing characters, to one of whom we give the greater
sympathy. In "The School" the tension is sustained, without
a real resolution, in a single character; though he may say,

        And what were dead Greek empires to me then?
        Dishonored, by Apollo, and forgot,

it is by his "Grecian thoughts" that he measures the new objects
of his devotion—the eyes that "would have sat in any witless
head," the "circumstantial" coin. We leave him facing like Janus
in two directions with a look of irony on each face—the kind
of irony we find in the mature poems.

In *Grace After Meat* Graves reprinted "The School," "The Lover," "Grace," "By the Riverside," "The Resurrection," "Under the Locusts," "The Cloak Model," "Wrestling," and a ninth poem, "Moonlight," which I have passed by here. This is the only reprinting from his first book that Ransom has permitted.

What first strikes the reader of *Poems About God* is the distance between it and *Selected Poems,* so wide that he may scarcely believe it the work of the same poet. But its themes, as I have noted, are those of the mature poems and so are the situations and the settings. And a third similarity, perhaps the most remarkable quality of *Poems About God* as a first book, is its anonymity. As a treatment—albeit a rather mechanical treatment—of various points of view, it has little of the auto-biographical quality we have come to expect in a modern writer's first volume. It would be some time before Ransom, working out his theory of poetry in his criticism, would declare anonymity "a condition of poetry." But his attitude to his art, as to life, was already fixed. His development in his subsequent volumes is a development largely in technique.

Chapter III

The Accomplished Poet: *Chills and Fever* and *Two Gentlemen in Bonds*

EXCEPT for two poems that might have been printed in *Poems About God* without being conspicuous by their style ("Fall of Leaf" and "The Vagrant," neither included in *Selected Poems*), Ransom's second book, *Chills and Fever*, is in his mature style. When Davidson, who admiringly had carried the early poems about with him in France in manuscript form, returned to Vanderbilt after the war, he found that Ransom in dissatisfaction "had taken a new turn" and was experimenting in the sonnet.

In fact he and [Walter Clyde] Curry had been engaged in a kind of sonnet *flyting*—firing strings of sonnets back and forth at one another in typescript. Ransom was apparently in the lead with what almost amounted to a sonnet sequence. Later, I believe, Ransom, still discontented, destroyed these numerous sonnets. I saw no more of them after a while, except the one or two that appear, remodelled, in his *Chills and Fever*.[1]

It was apparently during the second year of this experimenting that Ransom found his style, an occasion dated in Tate's memory by the composition of "Necrological" during the winter of 1921–22. This was the beginning of Ransom's brief but rich "major phase," a period that coincides almost exactly with the Fugitives' publication of their magazine from April, 1922, until December, 1925; *Chills and Fever* was published in 1924, thirty-

1. Davidson, p. 15.

six of its forty-nine poems having in fact first appeared in *The Fugitive*, and *Two Gentlemen in Bonds* was accepted for publication in the spring of 1926.

The titles of these two books are a dualist's kind of title. And the riddling young friar of "Necrological" might be called a monist at the point of turning into a dualist. His is the old debate of body and soul that had already occupied Ransom in his first book. That is a debate which presumably the friar would already have settled, and accordingly on this night he has "said his paternosters duly" and "scourged his limbs"; but his mind is "unruly," he cannot sleep, and at dawn he goes out from the monastery to face directly the cause of his trouble—a field still full of dead from a recent battle. He has his arguments ready: "it is easy he thought to die"; "heroes' flesh was thus. / Flesh fails";

> Bartholomew's stroke went home—but little it mattered,
> Bartholomew went to be stricken of other foemen.

Except as it is a trial to the soul, the friar is thinking, the body is irrelevant. Surely then the circumstances of death are irrelevant, and the disposition of the body afterward. But "beneath the blue ogive of the firmament," the foundation of what is lasting, the friar is bemused by what fails. The "gory" bodies are "fabulous," and it does seem to matter, as an insult to man, that they are eaten by "the grey wolf."

> Close by the sable stream that purged the plain
> Lay the white stallion and his rider thrown,
> The great beast had spilled there his little brain,
> And the little groin of the knight was spilled by a stone.

The body then is not merely an envelope; something of man's essence is there: even the seat of man's philosophy—the seat of the friar's own "deep surmise"—is an organ possessed in common by the beast.

Surely, too, since flesh fails, the friar has been right to give up his life to contemplation. But the postures of the dead knights tempt his imagination with another kind of life. There is another kind of devotion:

> a dead warrior, clutching whose mighty knees
> Was a leman, who with her flame had warmed his tent,
> For him enduring all men's pleasantries.

And there is a sword which he finds

> Deep in the belly of a lugubrious wight;
> He fingered it well, and it was cunningly made;
> But strange apparatus was it for a Carmelite.

When we leave the friar he is sitting with head bowed "as under a riddle," his dilemma unresolved,

> So still that he likened himself unto those dead
> Whom the kites of Heaven solicited with sweet cries.

It might have been made a gruesome scene, but Ransom keeps it at a distance by a phrase like "lugubrious wight," which ends a line whose beginning threatens the most homely kind of realism. "Deep in the belly of"—of no one in particular; of a vague entity denominated by a Latinism of humorous connotation modifying an archaism of Old English origin. (To the use of *wight* we know Ransom gave some study: he used it in the first published version of the poem in *The Fugitive,* substituted *knight* in *Chills and Fever,* and restored it in the only change he made in the poem for the Fugitives' anthology.) It is a distancing promised, as it were, by the title, although the word "Necrology," once used by newspapers as a euphemism for "Death Notices" (and still so used by PMLA), may keep for the reader trained like Ransom in the classical languages the particularity of its Greek root, *nekros,* "corpse." Even the description of the dead stallion and his thrown rider is not as graphic as it might be. We do not confront this whole battlefield of dead as directly as we confront the death of the single hired man who "in his vomit laid him down," in "Grace."

Another poem with a chivalric setting, "Armageddon" may be read as a kind of fable of the endless war between body and soul, represented by Antichrist, who enters the scene "playing his lissome flute and merry" ("lissome," apparently, to associate him with the serpent), and by Christ, who is "brooding upon his frugal breviary." They are knights, each with an army in his train, and at sight of each other they arm for battle. But Antichrist, whose motto might be "peace for our time," dismounts and doffs "his plume in generous prostration," Christ returns the courtesy, and they enter upon a knightly friendship. Cleverly—the poem reaches its limits in its cleverness, perhaps—Ransom contrasts their styles: Christ rides a "cynical hairy jennet" (*cynical* is meant in its now obsolete sense of "self-righteous"), Antichrist a Barbary steed; Antichrist carries "a spray of rosemary," Christ "a dry palm that grew on Calvary"; Christ wears "a dusty cassock," Antichrist owns a rich "tiringhall." After they exchange their mounts and rosemary and palm, Antichrist offers his new friend the use of his wardrobe,

> Whence Christ did not come forth too finical,
> But his egregious beauty richly dight.

(*Egregious* is obviously another word used with its older meanings in mind: "distinguished," "prominent.") At table Christ in his turn dilutes the wine to a "more ethereal bouquet." It seems an association from which both can only benefit, and indeed in their daily feasting and singing there seems a return to prelapsarian innocence (once, after all, "they were one brotherhood"). However, "it could not be." The Christian God does not quite harmonize with the pagan Dionysus:

> The rubric and the holy paternoster
> Were jangled strangely with the dithyramb.

An old patriarch who is disturbed by the misalliance seeks Christ's ear; because he can no longer tell the bosom friends apart, he speaks to Antichrist instead—"hissed in the wrong ear"—but the result is the same: Christ, shocked that such a mistake could be made, "sheds unmannerly his devil's pelf,"

> recalls his own to right opinions,
> With scourge they mortify their carnal selves.

And the war resumes between soul and body. "These Armageddons weary me much," says Antichrist, squeamish at the sight of blood, charming as spokesman for the claims of the body.

The carefully wrought and witty "Winter Remembered" is the only one among Ransom's selected poems that could be called a "love poem," though there are a number *about* lovers; but it is also a philosophical poem in its theme of the interdependence of soul and body, or of heart and body as the poem puts it. As a love poem it follows a somewhat devious route to pay a lady a compliment. The lover has spent a winter separated from her, but absence did not make *his* heart grow fonder, he says: his heart was "caked with cold, and past the smart of feeling." However, though the heart could not go on "dreaming" in the body's discomfort, the body was not independent of the heart, either; for it had had dignity and purpose only as a means of joining the lovers. Now his fingers were "idiot fingers," "frozen parsnips": far from his "cause," his "proper heat and center," the lover was no more than a vegetable. And that is a fair compliment.

For the usually conversational Ransom, "Winter Remembered" is somewhat declamatory; instead of understatement, there is exaggeration. Absence is a cry in the heart, winter is "furious," "murderous," the very air is frozen; the lover goes with eyeballs "streaming" and is minded of extreme remedies, of washing his wound in the snows. The first poem in *Selected Poems*, "Winter Remembered" stylistically opens the volume with a bang. But after all, we should not want a lover to mince his words; and for this lover, as for an old sergeant relating his combat experiences, it is safe to indulge himself a little, to speak of his "monstrous" suffering, because this is only a winter remembered, a separation successfully weathered: no need to exercise restraint for the sake of endurance. And this being Ransom, the exaggeration *is* kept within bounds. The biggest exaggeration and the largest compliment paid the lady is also a piece of wit that works against the pathetic:

> Dear love, these fingers that had known your touch,
> And tied our separate forces first together,
> Were ten poor idiot fingers not worth much,
> Ten frozen parsnips hanging in the weather.

The feminine rhymes are another means of lightening the tone. The poem's rhymes exhibit the kind of craftsmanship that poets hope their readers will notice, the scrolls meant for the eye as opposed to the joints meant to be hidden. In each stanza the first and third lines end in a masculine rhyme, the second and fourth lines in a feminine. Perhaps it was due to a little pride in this touch that the poet made certain each rhyme should be a "true" one: none of the slant rhymes with which he is free in other poems.

Something else of this poet's care we may observe in retracing the revisions of "Winter Remembered." It began as an English sonnet, the three quatrains essentially the same as the first three quatrains of the present version. ("Many a quatrain," remarked Frost, "is salvaged from a sonnet that went agley.")[2] Between the quatrain and the couplet the joint showed:

> Which would you choose, and for what boot in gold,
> The absence, or the absence and the cold?

For the second printed version Ransom dropped the couplet, inserted another quatrain after the first, and added the fourth and fifth quatrains of the present version. The inserted quatrain read:

> My winter's leave was much too cold for smarting,
> What bitter winds, and numbing snows and sorrows,
> And wheezy pines, like old men undeparting,
> To funeralize against all green young morrows!

Here both rhymes were feminine, breaking the pattern. The lines matched neither the extravagance of "A cry of Absence, Absence, in the heart," nor, in the comparison of pines to old men and in the directness of the phrase "all green young morrows!" the wit of the lines

> And though I think this heart's blood froze not fast
> It ran too small to spare one drop for dreaming.

And metrically, line four with its "funeralize" sounded flat in

2. "The Constant Symbol," introduction to *The Poems of Robert Frost* (New York: The Modern Library, 1946), p. xxi.

a poem strongly stressed. Ransom deleted the quatrain when he reprinted the poem in *Chills and Fever*. The fourth and fifth quatrains, however, fit perfectly with the earlier ones, clarifying and advancing the argument. The success Ransom has had with most of his own revisions seems to bear out his view of the importance of metre for the poet.

For the typical Ransom lovers, as in "Spectral Lovers," "Hilda," and "The Equilibrists," the soul never "descends," in the words of Donne, "to faculties"; the lovers are paralyzed by the opposing forces in their nature and can neither love nor abjure love. The "spectral lovers" remain only shadows of lovers, potential lovers, seen wandering homeless about the countryside at night in tortured attraction; *their* fingers are "fluttering like a bird / Whose song shall never be heard."

"Hilda" is a pair of sonnets Ransom restored to print, somewhat revised, in his *Selected Poems* of 1963, and it well deserves the reprinting. It was printed first in *Harper's Magazine* as a single sonnet titled "Ghosts," which corresponds to the present sonnet II. The ghosts belong apparently to women who could never bring themselves to love; now, lonely, regretful, guilty, they appear in the speaker's garden to cling about the quince bushes and roses, haunting the world of mortal beauty to which they had been afraid to commend themselves. They are unattractive apparitions, ascended as though from a part of hell kept for wasted lives: "blanched lepers," "a smoke / . . . smeared upon the skies"—images suggestive of waste. Yet they are "clamorous" to be remembered and loved and cry, " 'Do not spurn us.' " Of these the proudest is Hilda, "wreathing my roses with blue bitter dust."

Hilda had been the great beauty of the speaker's youth; as described in sonnet I,

> one to whom it fell
> To walk and wear her beauty as in a play
> To be enacted nobly on a great day;
> And stormily we approved the bosom-swell.

The speaker's wooing of her is described prettily in a way that parallels the garden scene of sonnet II:

>   For her touch and smell
> I brought bright flowers, till garlanded she stood
> Scared with her splendor, as in the sight of God
> A pale girl curtsying with an asphodel.

Hers was not merely the shyness of the young girls, but fear "as in the sight of God": the distrust of mortal love, "stormy" in its masculine expression, impure, and of mortal beauty, dangerous in its pride.

>   No, No, she answered in the extreme of fear,
>   I cannot.

On her "dropping of those petals / Rode the Estranger." This was to be her noble role, her "great day." Death heroically swept her up and away, not the lover. "I was a clod mumbling, to catch her ear." *Clod*, of course, is metaphorical in two senses: not only in the sense of "dullard," but also, more importantly, in the sense of "flesh."

In the second sonnet, however, the situation is reversed: Hilda becomes the suitor, her ghost seeking rest in the devotion of her old lover. This he would give, if he could. But what is there to which he can fasten his merely human love? His memory is of "the bosom swell" and "the tones tinkling." *He* is not all spirit, not yet; all smoke and "disbodied sigh." "But Hilda!" he addresses her, as though addressing a child, for she died without understanding:

>   Think not I would reject you, for I must
>   Weep for your nakedness and no retinue,
>   And leap up as of old to follow you;
>   But what I wear is flesh; it weighs like stone.

The final line corresponds to the final line of sonnet I: "I was a clod mumbling. . . ." But what he says at the end of sonnet I with the self-deprecation of the rejected suitor, he states at the end of the poem with the flatness of a definition, of a fact that may only be accepted.

The most significant revisions Ransom made in the sonnets for *Selected Poems* are in these two concluding lines. In *Two Gentlemen in Bonds* the concluding line of sonnet I read simply:

"I was such earth as whispered in her ear." The word *earth* fit the theme well enough—too obviously, perhaps—but did not fit the feelings of the rejected lover nearly as well as *clod*. And in *whispering* there was a suggestion of the serpent's whispering to Eve that Ransom may have decided was not quite to the point, if the point was to be not guilt but the lover's hopeless clumsiness, as he feels, before Hilda's ethereality. So he describes himself as a "clod mumbling." The concluding line of sonnet II originally read: "But flesh hath monstrous gravity, as of stone." The theme is brought to a sharper focus by the dualism implicit in the word *wear*. And the rhythm is better fitted to the sense by the stresses on the three final syllables:

$$\breve{\text{it}}\ \acute{\text{weighs}}\ |\ \grave{\text{like}}\ \acute{\text{stone.}}$$

That is, a secondary stress on *like*, primary stresses on *weighs* and *stone*.

This is a brilliant pair of sonnets, in conception, in phrasing. It would be reading too much by the sweat of our brows to try to explain each time the effect of the felicitous phrase, but one more line here is worth examining: "And stormily we approved the bosom-swell." We might imagine a gathering of young men talking about the town beauty. In the word *approved* is a little of the condescension of the young male, who pretends perhaps to have somewhat more choice among the women than he really has. In this case as it turns out he has none. "Stormily" the young men approve: sincerely passionate, no doubt, but in each other's company a little too eager to have full credit for their manhoods. The town beauty, though, is described in a rather formal phrase: *"the* [not *her*] bosom-swell." And Ransom declines a more anatomical word, or even *bosom* by itself, but bosom-*swell*—suggestion, potential, a promise never kept.

Finally, a word on these sonnets as sonnets. Ransom once said humorously that he prints his sonnets with a break between octave and sestet in order to "disguise" them, sonnets being presently out-of-fashion.[3] But rather than disguise them, his

3. Reading at Belmont College, Nashville, 1961. The practice, of course, is not peculiar to Ransom.

practice calls attention with perhaps a little pride to the logic of their form. In his interesting essay "Shakespeare at Sonnets," he has written:

> The metrical pattern of any sonnet is directive. If the English sonnet exhibits the rhyme-scheme ABAB CDCD EFEF GG, it imposes upon the poet the following requirement: that he write three coordinate quatrains and then a couplet which will relate to the series collectively.
>
> .   .   .   .   .
>
> It is not every matter, or logical object, which allows this [three-and-one division]; and, particularly, the couplet does not give enough room for the comment unless the burden of the quatrains has been severely restricted. If the poet is too full of urgent thoughts, he had better use the two-part or Italian form, which is very much more flexible.[4]

What of Ransom himself at the sonnet? Though he speaks of the Italian sonnet's greater flexibility, he himself keeps the two parts strictly separate, never allowing the syntax or the thought of the octave to spill over into the sestet. In sonnet I of "Hilda," the octave treats the young men's admiration and the speaker's wooing, the sestet treats her response; in sonnet II the octave treats the ghosts in general, the sestet Hilda in particular with a turn in the thought announced by the first words, "But Hilda!" In each sonnet in *Selected Poems* (each one is Italian), the sestet is marked at the least by such a turn.

From one significant standpoint, the importance Ransom places on the metrical pattern of the sonnet is exaggerated. When a sonnet is read aloud to us—and the hearing of a poem would have to be our most intense experience of it—we do not notice at which line the turn of thought is effected, in the case of the Italian sonnet: we hear only that a turn is made; in the case of the English sonnet, we may hear the co-ordination of the quatrains when it is a matter of parallel syntax as in Shakespeare's sonnet 64, "When I have seen by Time's fell hand defaced," each of whose quatrains begins with a *when* clause. But when there is no co-ordination, our ears do not miss it.

4. *The World's Body,* pp. 273, 275.

Our ears do not hear the sonnet itself, as a *form*. They are indifferent to the formal differences between an Italian sonnet and, say, one of Meredith's sixteen-line "sonnets": before the end of the poem is reached, they have forgotten the number of the lines, they have forgotten rhymes. Probably the ballad stanza, with its short lines, is about as much poetic form as our ears can take in. The logic Ransom obeys in his sonnets matters only on the page.

Ransom's most famous lovers are definitely his "Equilibrists." This poem is untypical in its lack of a clear dramatic or narrative situation (the poem was at first mistitled somewhat, it would seem, as "*History* of Two Simple Lovers"). It begins with a clear enough situation: the man "alone in the press of people," remembering the woman's beauty but also "the cruel words" unspoken between them but in both their minds—"Honor, Honor"; and so the unspoken command,

> Arise,
> Leave me now, and never let us meet,
> Eternal distance now command thy feet.

We could imagine something like the previous marriage of one that makes honor as powerful a force as their love and keeps them in a "torture of equilibrium." It appears that, though they never forget each other, they never meet again. But at the end of the poem circumstances are not clear enough for us to piece out a story. The forsworn lovers have somehow come to be buried side by side, and it is the poet himself who fashions their common tomb—or is his poem their tomb, as in Donne's lines from "The Canonization"?

> We'll build in sonnets pretty rooms;
> As well a well-wrought urn becomes
> The greatest ashes, as half-acre tombs.

Clearly, the poem is concerned not with a "real" action, but with a representative situation. It is about "the history of love in western literature and society," an English critic has said;

"Ransom's two lovers are archetypes, like Tristan and Iseult, or Aucassin and Nicolette, or Paolo and Francesca."[5]

"Simple lovers," Ransom first called them. It may seem an odd epithet: they are anything but simple, in the sense of *uncomplicated,* else they would have no problem.

> Predicament indeed, which thus discovers
> Honor among thieves, Honor between lovers.

All is fair in love and war. It is, of course, in the sense of *innocent* and *honest* that they are simple: unwilling to compromise their natures, they can be neither cynical, and deny honor, nor moral and practical, and deny each other. At first the poet feels regret for them in their predicament, as for Hilda and the spectral lovers.

> Ah, the strict lovers, they are ruined now!
> I cried in anger.

However, they do not decline love, like those others, partly out of fear. Although they would be objects of ridicule or scorn to the cynic and the moralist—"gibbeted" is the word the poet uses—in their impossible dual allegiance they are courageous. So in the next half-line the poet's tone begins to shift:

> But with puddled brow
> Devising for those gibbeted and brave
> Came I descanting . . .

The point of the self-deprecation—the "puddled brow," the mock-grandiloquent "descanting"—is that the poet does not pretend to have all of the answers; he merely devises, he in fact can only ask a question:

> Man, what would you have?
> For spin your period out, and draw your breath,
> A kinder saeculum begins with Death.
> Would you ascend to Heaven and bodiless dwell?
> Or take your bodies honorless to Hell?

5. Bernard Bergonzi, "A Poem About the History of Love," *Critical Quarterly,* IV, No. 2 (Summer, 1962), 137.

The lovers' predicament is man's predicament. Their "Epitaph" accordingly is a quatrain of unqualified eloquence and beauty— unqualified by any of the means with which Ransom usually complicates his tone:

> Equilibrists lie here; stranger, tread light;
> Close, but untouching in each other's sight;
> Mouldered the lips and ashy the tall skull.
> Let them lie perilous and beautiful.

From Ransom, it is almost a piece of "pure poetry."

" 'This life is not good but in danger and joy,' " thinks the Grandfather in "Old Man Playing with Children," as he dances in an Indian costume around a backyard bonfire with his grandsons. His thoughts recall those of "The Christian" in *Poems About God*.

> "Do not offer your reclining-chair and slippers
> With tedious old women talking in wrappers."

Grandfather is addressing his son or his son-in-law, a "discreet householder" naturally fearful that his house will catch fire, and others of the middle generation " 'who are penned as slaves by properties and causes.' "

> "May God forgive me, I know your middling ways,
> Having taken care and performed ignominies unreckoned
> Between the first brief childhood and the brief second,
> But I will be more honorable in these days."

Although his treatment of the theme in its lightness and restraint might be called "classical," this is a somewhat romantic vein running through Ransom: the "middling ways" and other ways in which men and women waste their powers, lose their lives in trying to save them. In "Morning" the way is rationalism and practicality. Ralph is awakened one morning to a vision of the lambent beauty beyond his window, in the meadow, and to a vision of a heightened kind of life with his wife Jane; it is described as an almost religious awakening: the silence is

"blessed," and he is about to "propose to Jane" not, as before,
a dull partnership, but a little miracle, that they "go walking / Through the green waves" of clover. But suddenly

> His manliness returned entire to Ralph;
> The dutiful mills of the brain
> Began to whir with their smooth-grinding wheels.

And it becomes "simply another morning, and simply Jane."
Or in "Old Man Pondered" it is simply fear of pain and disappointment that has kept an old man on lifelong guard against
the emotions, either of love or of hate; though he has gotten
through life unharmed from without, an impressive figure for
his age, he is dead in spirit, his eye "monstered in its fixed in-
tent" on "his own predicament."

Ransom's best known poem on the theme is "Good Ships,"
one of his finest sonnets. Except for one line, each detail of
the poem is fitted to the one metaphor, and gracefully. The
man and woman, the "good ships," meet "on the high seas"—in
high society, as the metaphor translates—"on the loud
surge / Of one of Mrs. Grundy's Tuesday teas." They are "good"
as we mean boys and girls are good—"So seaworthy one felt
they could not sink": sink socially, sink to an unseemly show
of the attraction that the poet thinks two such "fleet ships"
must feel. They exchange the small talk of their society, "the
nautical technicalities," and part forever, "most certainly
bound" for the safety, and dullness, of "port." "Still there was
a tremor shook them, I should think," the poet offers modestly,

> Beautiful timbers fit for storm and sport
> And unto miserly merchant hulks converted.

It is not an aristocratic code that rules them; their society is
not aristocratic in any sense, but merely a modern commercial
society. The good ships travel only the trade routes.

In the changes he made in the poem after its first printing,
Ransom had chiefly the metaphor in mind. The second line originally read: "Who speak, and unto eternity diverge." He changed
the overly explicit "unto eternity" to the more maritime "unto
the vast." In line 13, quoted above, he changed *meant* to *fit*,

which goes better with *timbers.* In the same line, incidentally, it is interesting to note his change of "stormy sport" to "storm and sport," characteristic of his fondness for dichotomies. But line four remains untamed: "A macaroon absorbed all her emotion"; it is an unseaman-like biscuit, however watery *absorbed* may sound.

The bride of "In Process of a Noble Alliance" could well be the lady of "Good Ships." It is a *mariage de convenance,* and her youth and beauty, lost to life—

> For now in funeral white they lead her
> And crown her queen of the House of No Love

—are fit only to be the subject of a tombstone sculpture: "Reduce this lady unto marble quickly"; of a photograph for the society pages: "Ray her beauty on a glassy plate"; or of an elegy: "Rhyme her youth as fast as the granite." The poem is elegant but slight, and I wonder whether its eight lines were quatrains of a sonnet for which there was insufficient matter for fourteen lines, its rhyme scheme altered to disguise its origin.

The chivalric metaphor of "Spectral Lovers" and "The Equilibrists," which makes the body "that marble fortress not to be conquered" or "a white field" guarded by the "gaunt tower" of the head, is put to more humorous use in the title "Emily Hardcastle, Spinster." This poem is light though it ends in Emily's death, for its subject is really a kind of double joke. Emily is a small-town aristocrat who, "finer" than her sisters, would not be satisfied by marrying a merchant as they did or in fact by marrying any of the local young men. The young men, however, remained confident.

> We were only local beauties, and we beautifully trusted
> If the proud one had to tarry we would have her by default.

The joke is on them, for "right across her threshold has her Grizzled Baron come." But the final joke, a terrible joke, is of course on Emily Hardcastle, for her deliverer is death.

> Let them wrap her as a princess, who'd go softly down a
>   stairway
> And seal her to the stranger for his castle in the gloom.

"Grizzled" is the first hint, the ambiguity of "wrap" a second, and "seal" and "castle in the gloom" the certain indications that "the stately ceremonial" announced in the first stanza is not to be a wedding. Yet the tone of these two lines—"Let them wrap her as a princess"—is, I think, somewhat tender. For the speaker knows Emily to be partly right in holding out for someone better; his acknowledgement shows in the humorous way he remembers himself—"I was dapper when I dangled in my pepper-and-salt"—and the other "local beauties." Let her death then be what her life was not.

The distinctiveness of this poem lies somewhere in the sound, to which more than anything else is due the effect of lightness that allows one to speak in terms of "jokes." The meter is the fourteener popular in the sixteenth century:

> We shall come | to mor | row morn | ing, || who | were not |
> to have | her love,
> We shall bring | no face | of en | vy || but | a gift |
> of praise | and lil | ies
> To the state | ly ce | re mo | ni al || we | are not |
> the he | roes of.

But further comment is necessary. Only three of the lines are regular fourteeners—two of these in the final stanza, in which the "Grizzled Baron" enters to a kind of iambic march:

> But right | a cross | her thresh | hold has | her Griz |
> zled Bar | on come.

In the other lines there are anapaestic substitutions and feminine endings. Moreover, the effect of the caesura—bound to be strongly marked in lines of this length—is to lend a generally anapaestic movement to lines in which the fourth stress is not strong, the reason being that in every line the caesura comes in the middle, after the third stress. In fact, in every line but two the caesura comes precisely in the middle: in lines of fifteen or sixteen syllables it comes after the eighth (except for line three scanned above); in the fourteeners it comes after the seventh (except for line seven: "I was dapper when I dangled || in my pepper-and-salt"). Since the caesura splits the line in effect into two half-lines, we have a desire, if the first syllable after the caesura is not rhetorically important, to read the second half as metrically like the first and give it only three stresses. In the first line, for example, we are tempted to pass over *who*, which is only lightly stressed, and read the line this way:

We shall come | to mor | row morn ing, ||| who were not |
to have | her love,

This time I have marked the third foot as an amphibrach out of respect to the strong caesura. In the following line we may even more easily pass over the conjunction:

We were on | ly lo | cal beau ties, ||| and we beau |
ti ful | ly trust | ed

There are of course other effects, more easily defined, that contribute to the lightness of the verse. Stresses are segregated throughout, there being neither the hovering stresses nor the juxtaposition of primary stresses that are often found in Ransom's poems. And there is a good deal of alliteration, as in stanza two: "who are red-eyed, who are wroth"; "she was finer, for they wearied of the waiting / And they married them to merchants, being unbelievers both."

Another of the poems that I am calling "romantic" is "Dog," one of Ransom's several little animal fables. It may seem at first puzzlingly pointless: the dog baits a prize bull, the master arrives and beats him home to his kennel. Like "Morning," the poem appeared in "The Manliness of Men" section of *Two Gentlemen in Bonds*. In this instance it is manliness in its positive sense that is represented, by the bull; and the effete, the over-civilized, is represented by the dog,

> A pretty little creature with tears in his eyes
> And anomalous hand extended on his leg;
> Housebroken was my Huendchen, and so wise.
>
> Booms the voice of a big dog like a bell.
> But Fido sits at dusk on Madam's lap
> And, bored beyond his tongue's poor skill to tell,
> Rehearses his pink paradigm, To yap.

His yapping, moreover, is in a moralistic vein, a "monologue" delivered "with a lion's courage and a bee's virulence." Ransom's theme was clearer in a stanza he dropped from the *Selected Poems* version: to the terrible cry of the bull interrupted on his way to his adoring wives, "What do you want of my twenty lady kine?" was answered,

> Ah, nothing doubtless; yet his dog's fang is keen,
> His dog's heart cannot suffer these marriage rites
> Enacted in the dark if they are obscene;
> Misogynist, censorious of delights.

When the outraged bull charges, the dog proves too mean an enemy for proper battle:

>   his horn
> Slices the young birch into splinter and shank
> But lunging leaves the bitch's boy untorn.

It is a scene of extreme indignity for the bull "of gentle pedigree," and he is left weeping among his ladies. But the dog, whipped back to his kennel, has not spent his malice, and the final description of him is ominous:

> God's peace betide the souls
> Of the pure in heart! But in the box that fennel
> Grows round, are two red eyes that stare like coals.

Portrait of the moralist as a young dog: obviously it is not in a pure heart that his moralism has its source, but in something like the dangerous *ressentiment* of which Nietzsche speaks so much as the deepest motive of the weak and the mean-spirited in the presence of the noble and strong (represented in our fable by the pedigreed bull). This must be the reason for the "terror" of which the poet speaks in the opening stanza:

> Cock-a-doodle-doo the brass-lined rooster says,
> Brekekekex intones the fat Greek frog—
> These fantasies do not terrify me as
> The bow-wow-wow of dog.

Ransom's major theme, as I have said, is mortality, the theme in one way or another of most of his better-known poems: "Bells for John Whiteside's Daughter," "Here Lies a Lady," "Dead Boy," "Janet Waking," "Blue Girls," "Piazza Piece."

When Ransom writes of death he keeps it at a distance by keeping its victim at distance, as we have seen in "Necrological": not at a "safe distance," but at a dignified distance. And he keeps the bereaved at a distance too, when these take the death hard, as in "Dead Boy," or he shows even the bereaved keeping a stern self-control. Robert Penn Warren's analysis of the way these effects are obtained through the diction and phrasing in "Bells for John Whiteside's Daughter" is well known.[6]

The poem's somewhat prosy rhythm has also been pointed to as a means by which a too-obvious pathos is avoided. ("Every time I reprint my poems I tinker with them—and especially towards tightening up the meters. But I never wanted to tinker with this one,"[7] Ransom has said.) The most distinctive feature of its rhythm though, I think, is the long period in the middle; it begins with the second line of stanza two and lasts to the end of stanza four, with three consecutive run-on lines in stanza four and no internal pauses within that stanza.

6. A part of "Pure and Impure Poetry," *The Kenyon Review*, V, No. 2 (Spring, 1943), 228–254.
7. *Conversations* . . . , p. 22.

> We looked among orchard trees and beyond
> Where she took arms against her shadow,
> Or harried unto the pond
>
> The lazy geese, like a snow cloud
> Dripping their snow on the green grass,
> Tricking and stopping, sleepy and proud,
> Who cried in goose, Alas,
>
> For the tireless heart within the little
> Lady with rod that made them rise
> From their noon apple-dreams and scuttle
> Goose-fashion under the skies!

It is appropriate to the pleasurable sweep of the memory that ends abruptly at the stern fact of the present: "But now go the bells, and we are ready."[8]

However, Ransom's distant tone in "Here Lies a Lady," the poem that furnished the title *Chills and Fever*, has caused a good deal of puzzlement.

The poem ends with an attitude so devoid of emotion that it is disconcerting. First, the address to the "Sweet ladies" is so impersonal that we utterly lose touch with a specific personality who had suffered an illness leading to death. The archaic language and the self-conscious rhetoric increase the already excessive aloofness. Then comes the bizarre question, "But was she not lucky?" . . . Ransom chooses to end the poem with a tone so cold that it seems non-human. This may be consistent with the poem's many detached and objective effects, but it seems like a contrived flight from the legitimate human emotion that we are invited to share in the second stanza. In combatting the sentimental elegy Ransom has been caught in the counter-trap of callousness and non-human detachment.

Is the lady lucky to be relieved of the oscillations between pointless fury and cold inertness? Is she lucky to die with people around to mourn? Is she lucky to have so symmetrical a death? *She* did not bloom long; *she* did not thole toughly.[9]

8. The long period and the enjambment make the middle stanzas difficult to read aloud. Ransom's most recent recorded reading of the poem is far from his best because he runs short of breath in the middle. The record is "John Crowe Ransom Reads from His Own Works," Yale Series of Recorded Poets (New York: Decca Records, 1966), made in 1961.

9. Thornton H. Parsons, "The Civilized Poetry of John Crowe Ransom," *Perspective*, XIII, No. 4 (Autumn, 1964), 251. The poem has also been the subject of several speculations in *The Explicator*.

Indeed it is difficult to know how to take the tone of this poem, and I offer my comment only after recourse at some points to Ransom's recorded reading of it.

"Here lies a lady of beauty and high degree," the first line announces, as though we were standing before a monument in a reflective mood, prepared to trace a paradigm in the life of one of high estate. But the principle behind this life we do not find very profound: the lady was "the delight," like a child or pet, equally of a husband, an aunt, an infant (with whom we would expect the relationship to be the reverse), and the doctors, irreverently called "medicos," who in "marvelling sweetly on her ills" remind us a little of the kites with their "sweet cries" at the end of "Necrological."

> Of chills and fever she died, of fever and chills,
> The delight of her husband, her aunt, an infant of three,
> And of medicos marvelling sweetly on her ills.

Even her death is irreverently described in sing-song, and "fever" uncovers a pun in the first line on "high degree." The point of her life seems to be a pointless death.

The irreverence of the first stanza does not make impossible a pathetic tone in the second and third stanzas, however; that is the way Ransom reads them himself. Line seven—"What was she making? Why, nothing . . ."—could be read in a detached tone, but Ransom reads it in a tone of sympathy and pity. The lady, after all, does die, and her death comes after a disturbingly undignified illness:

> For either she burned, and her confident eyes would blaze,
> And her fingers fly in a manner to puzzle their heads—
> What was she making? Why, nothing; she sat in a maze
> Of old scraps of laces, snipped into curious shreds—
>
> Or this would pass, and the light of her fire decline
> Till she lay discouraged and cold, like a thin stalk white
>   and blown.

Is there any significance in her strange alteration between chills and fever? Life itself is a kind of sickness, as the existentialist tells us, and the lady's manner of dying epitomizes what for Ransom is the nature of it: unresolvable war between spirit and body, between chilly reason and feverish emotion. Perhaps in the number of her chills and fever—six of each, adding to twelve—we are even meant to think of the year-cycle, and thus the life-cycle: as though, dying early in her wifehood and motherhood, she should experience the baffling essence of a complete human life in her "six little spaces of chill, and six of burning."

In the final stanza Ransom abruptly shifts the tone once again with his bizarre question. The question, though, is in the first place of the simplest kind of irony: the kind in which meaning is the direct opposite of the words, as when one asks, soaked with rain, "Isn't *this* a nice day?"

> Sweet ladies, long may ye bloom, and toughly I hope ye may
>   thole,
> But was she not lucky?

The question would be ironic, and startling, asked in any words, but it is especially so in the word *lucky*. Compared to its synonyms, the word is somewhat vulgar in many of its usages, as in the expression "down on his luck." In D. H. Lawrence's story "The Rocking Horse Winner," for example, it becomes confused in the boy's mind with *lucre*. Horse players may be lucky, or people who just catch the last bus home, before it rains; ladies of beauty and high degree, the delights of their husbands, aunts, and infants of three, are blessed, or fortunate—anyway, not lucky, except to the most vulgar imagination, the kind that is entertained by the lives, and deaths, of the movie stars. Only such an imagination would fasten on the "flowers and lace and mourning" that decorate the lady's passing, thinking of how different the very rich are from the rest of us, how "lucky." The significance of the irony becomes clear in Ransom's own reading of line 14. Instead of what one may think to be the meter of the first two feet,

$$\breve{\text{Bu}}\text{t wa}\acute{\text{s}} \mid \text{she no}\acute{\text{t}}\, \text{luck} \mid \breve{\text{y}}?$$

Ransom reads it

But was she | not luck | y?

That is to ask, "Was *she* not different from you ordinary (though likewise sweet) ladies, to whom it is only given toughly to endure, don't you envy her?" What can the ladies answer? "Why, *no,* she died, just as we will die someday, and the ceremony and the honor they pay her do not seem to matter as they should. The ceremony does not seem satisfying, somehow. You leave us at a loss, Mr. Ransom, as to what *does* matter."

And that is the point. Life and death are seen in this poem not even as a mystery, but as a little puzzle, like the maze of laces in which the lady sits when in her feverish state. Before such a puzzle our rituals seem grand but clumsy devices:

> In flowers and lace and mourning,
> In love and great honor we bade God rest her soul
> After six little spaces of chill, and six of burning.

In his reading Ransom pronounces *soul* with ironic over-emphasis (its rhyme with the bookish *thole* is just a little playful), as he does other of the nouns above, like *honor*: as though to say, where is there *soul* in any of this? We see no emanation of the soul in her superficial life, and none in the ludicrous reactions of her dying body. We look to the life of an aristocratic lady expecting there to be meaning, because there is order, and there is none. For the traditionalist, ceremony is a source of meaning, ceremony transcends the circumstance.

> How but in custom and in ceremony
> Are innocence and beauty born?
> (W. B. Yeats, "A Prayer for My Daughter")

That we know is Ransom's attitude generally. But Ransom can look at this matter, as at every other, in two ways. "My objects as a poet might be something like the following," he wrote to Tate in 1927, when he had begun to grow a critic's consciousness of his own verse: "(1) I want to find the experience that is in the common actuals; (2) I want this experience to carry (by association, of course) the dearest possible values to which we have attached ourselves; (3) I want to face the disintegration or nullification of these values as calmly and religiously as possible."[10]

A ceremony is after all a human institution and subject to failures; in this instance there is a large disparity between the ceremony and the circumstance that the ceremony does not transcend or "explain." The poem's effect is exactly opposite to that of Yeats's "Upon a Dying Lady." In its theme Ransom's poem may more likely be compared to the conclusion of Graham Greene's novel *The Heart of the Matter,* in which the Church, after Lt. Scobie's death, is seen even by the priest as a poor human gesture toward explaining the unexplainable.

Thematically, we are left at the end of "Here Lies a Lady" simply with the fact of life and the fact of death. (I say "thematically," for the poem itself, as a *formal* experience, does make death yield somewhat to our demand that events make "sense," our refusal to be overwhelmed by them. Frost's definition of poetry as "a momentary stay against confusion" comes to mind.) In the final line therefore the tone of irony gives way again to the pathetic—especially, as Ransom reads it, in the last word, *burning.* The poem is the most complicated in tone of all of Ransom's poems; but Ransom's reading makes "tonal sense" of it.

In "Dead Boy," which to a degree also involves a failure of ceremony, we can count five ways of viewing the death. There is the purely objective view: "He was pale and little, the foolish neighbors say." The view is conveyed by the title itself—"dead boy," object, one of a class; by the businesslike metaphors of death, "subtraction" and "transaction"; by the very tone the speaker takes in a phrase like "the world of outer dark":

> And none of the county kin like the transaction,
> Nor some of the world of outer dark, like me.

But the purely objective or practical viewpoint is held only by

10. March, 1927, quoted in Louise Cowan, *The Fugitive Group: A Literary History* (Baton Rouge: Louisiana State University Press, 1959), p. 178.

the "foolish neighbors"; the speaker's viewpoint, while objective, is also understanding and sympathetic.

> A pig with a pasty face, so I had said,
> Squealing for cookies, kinned by poor pretense
> With a noble house. But the little man quite dead,
> I see the forbears' antique lineaments.

The tone of the second sentence, "But the little man quite dead . . . ," as Ransom reads it, is not a tone of revelation, but of concession, so that there is no development in the speaker's attitude: the speaker instead keeps his dual viewpoint.

These are the objective viewpoints. The subjective viewpoints are that of the mother: "never / Woman bewept her babe as this is weeping" (but the verb the poet assigns her, *bewept*, keeps her at a distance); and, very different from hers, that of the Virginia patriarchs, who are "hurt with a deep dynastic wound." And last, there is the religious viewpoint: "The first-fruits, saith the Preacher, the Lord hath taken." Ideally, the religious viewpoint becomes the inclusive viewpoint. But the grief of the elder men, on which the poem focuses, is not reconciled to the large view. Much of their situation and their feeling tells in the single word *strode* in the next-to-last stanza:

> The elder men have strode by the box of death
> To the wide flag porch, and muttering low send round
> The bruit of the day.

The word suggests the long limbs of the men of the "noble house"—though sapless now—their habit of decisive movement, the wide-legged movement perhaps of horsemen—in a word, the strength which will end with them and to which the boy, "pale and little," would probably not have succeeded anyway had he lived. And the word implies their impatience with the ceremony of death, which does not console them; for

> this was the old tree's late branch wrenched away,
> Grieving the sapless limbs, the shorn and shaken.

The one poem that is, I think, unsuccessful in its treatment of death is "Puncture." It has been extravagantly praised, apparently because it offers something of the circumstantiality of prose fiction. But I find Ransom's values stated in this poem rather too obviously. Here the stern control is not expressed through a single word like *vexed* that is, as Warren says, a ritual word—no one would literally say above the coffin of a child, "I am vexed." The control is expressed in the speeches and manner of Grimes, the dying soldier who does not want his comrade to fuss over him, and more in the speeches than in the manner:

> "Get away. Go work on the corpses, if you wish,
> Prop their heads up again, wrap their bones in,
> They were good pious men.

> "But as for me I have the devil's desire
> For delicate tobacco in my pipe, and leisure
> To stretch my toes in comfort by this fire.
> Amuse yourself then some way, find some pleasure
> Sleeping, or digging a treasure."

Grimes talks too much. Could we call it an overstated understatement? I cannot quite believe in him as I could were he to speak only his one sentence in stanza three, which answers the narrator's first offer to tend his wound: " 'No, it's an old puncture,' said Grimes, / 'Which takes to bleeding sometimes.' " Then there would be a soldierly taciturnity to go with the manly understatement of "puncture." This is a quality in fact that is suggested of Grimes by the final stanza, a passage of a much higher order than Grimes's long speech:

> Blue blazed the eyes of Grimes in the old manner—
> The flames of eyes which jewel the head of youth
> Were strange in the leathery phiz of the old campaigner—
> Smoke and a dry word crackled from his mouth
> Which a cold wind ferried south.

And the narrator himself talks too much:

> "Why, Grimes, I never knew your mortal blood
> Had wasted for my sake in scarlet streams,
> And no word said. A curse on my manhood
> If I knew anything! This is my luck which seems
> Worse than my evillest dreams."

These speeches make the middle of the poem overlong and loose, in contrast to the graceful economy of the final stanza, above, and of the opening stanzas:

> Darkness was bad as weariness, till Grimes said,
> "We've got to have a fire." But in that case
> The match must sputter and the flame glare red
> On nothing beautiful, and set no seal of grace
> On any dead man's face.
>
> And when the flames roared, when the sparks dartled
> And quenched in the black sea that closed us round,
> I looked at Grimes my dear comrade and startled
> His look, blue-bright—and under it a wound
> Which bled upon the ground.

The subject of "Piazza Piece" is not an actual death but a future death; or better, it is the constant presence of death in life as a young girl becomes half aware of it. She is waiting for her "truelove," but it is an incomplete reading of the poem to think of her simply as excessively romantic—as any more romantic than the next young girl. The setting is the "archetypal" love scene. It is Capulet's orchard, as Juliet on her balcony first becomes aware that her words have been overheard:

> But what man art thou that thus bescreen'd in night
> So stumblest on my counsel?

But it is not her Romeo that Ransom's Juliet discovers eavesdropping:

> But what grey man among the vines is this
> Whose words are dry and faint as in a dream?

It is, of course, Death. Notice that the title itself (*piazza* means *porch* in the South) invites the ironic comparison to Shakespeare's Italian setting. Here are two other comparisons:

> Because I could not stop for Death,
> He kindly stopped for me. . . .

.   .   .   .   .

> "Tell me, thou bonny bird,
>   When shall I marry me?"
> "When six braw gentlemen
>   Kirkward shall carry ye."
>
> "Who makes the bridal bed,
>   Birdie, say truly?"—
> "The grey-headed sexton
>   That delves the grave duly."

That is, Juliet is as naturally absorbed in her young girl's dream of life as Emily Dickinson's lady is absorbed in her busy days (in both poems Death is a gentleman suitor, driving a carriage in Dickinson's poem and in Ransom's an early automobile, for which he wears, significantly, a "dustcoat"); and Juliet is no more to be blamed as excessively romantic for wanting "the young men's whispering and sighing" than is Scott's Proud Maisie as excessively proud: they have only the usual expectations of beautiful young girls. Theirs are to be denied so finally as to suggest the most terribly ironic metaphors: the grave as a bridal bed, death as an aged lover.

But I see the possibility of a richer significance that Ransom's poem shares with Hardy's "Heiress and Architect." The heiress wishes the architect to build her a mansion with many openings onto the beauties of nature; but he rejects her plan as idle, "for winters freeze." She asks for a more practical but equally cheerful house, with something like picture windows, but he says no again. And he says no to her idea for a little love chamber, "for you will fade." Finally she asks,

>   "O, contrive some way—
> Some narrow winding turret, quite mine own,
> To reach a loft where I may grieve alone!
> It is a slight thing; hence do not, I pray,
>   This last dear fancy slay!"
>
>   "Such winding ways
>   Fit not your days,"
> Said he, the man of measuring eye;
> "I must even fashion as the rule declares,

> To wit: Give space (since life ends unawares)
> To hale a coffined corpse adown the stairs;
> For you will die."[11]

Ransom's grey man takes a more gentle and understanding tone:

> Your ears are soft and small
> And listen to an old man not at all,
> They want the young men's whispering and sighing.

His lesson, though, is just as cruel:

> But see the roses on your trellis dying
> And hear the spectral singing of the moon.

Let us imagine that Juliet's expectations are fulfilled: that her truelove does come, that they marry, that they even raise a family. But Death can wait, and meanwhile Juliet, like Hardy's heiress, must feel his presence at every turn. Nor does Death have to wait long, relatively speaking: "I must have my lovely lady soon."

Although Death is a somewhat disreputable gentleman, given to eavesdropping, his speech like the young lady's is quite formal. It is this formality that gives the poem its special quality. He speaks the octave, she the sestet, in accordance with Ransom's strict view of sonnet structure; so there are two set speeches, rather than a dialogue. "I am a gentleman in a dustcoat trying / To make you hear," he begins. This first line is repeated in the eighth line to close his speech with the same formality, but this time there is no grammatical object for *trying*: "I am a gentleman in a dustcoat trying." The reader may not only supply the object from the second line, he may also supply a sexual connotation to *trying*, as in Marvell's lines: "then worms shall try / That long preserved virginity." The lady in her turn formally introduces herself: "I am a lady young in beauty waiting / Until my truelove comes." It is in her speech that we realize the identity of the formal old gentleman, as she herself does not; and our identification comes with a little shock of horror

11. This poem seems to be a favorite of Ransom himself. I judge from the lectures he gave on Hardy while a visiting professor at Vanderbilt during 1961-62. He included it in his *Selected Poems of Thomas Hardy.*

because the reality is half hidden behind the formal, even stilted speeches, behind the tone of ladylike affront—"Back from my trellis, Sir, before I scream." Her final line, like his, repeats the introduction without an object: "I am a lady young in beauty waiting." All that she is waiting for—all that is awaiting her—she does not yet, in a full sense, know.

I have called the old gentleman's lesson cruel; but it is the knowledge of death, knowledge deeper than a kind of textbook understanding that man is mortal, that one must arrive at before he may begin to live with the widest awareness. This is the ultimate theme of the confrontations that Ransom arranges between innocence and knowledge: in "Miriam Tazewell," in "Vaunting Oak," "Parting at Dawn," "Janet Waking," "Blue Girls." These poems are all concerned with lessons. The child Janet "would not be instructed in how deep / Was the forgetful kingdom of death." The girl in "Vaunting Oak" had already "been instructed of much mortality," but being "wrapped in a phantasy of good," imagining the old oak a fit symbol of lasting love, required "that her pitiful error be undone." In the non-narrative and the non-dramatic poems, the tone of the poet himself is one of patient instruction. In the second stanza of "Miriam Tazewell"—she has kept her innocence long and is frightened "like a young thing"—he shifts the point-of-view to address Miriam directly:

> But the earth shook dry his old back in good season,
> He had weathered storms that drenched him deep as this
>   one,
> And the sun, Miriam, ascended to his dominion,
> The storm was withered against his empyrean.

In "Parting at Dawn" he again adopts an older poet's setting. But instead of the "path of gold" that stretches straight in Browning's poem, there is "the cold glitter of light" in which "stoics are born." The goddess invoked in this sonnet is not Love but Philosophy, who teaches that all things must end, love included. The little death of parting anticipates the death of love itself, which will survive neither the world of men, to which Browning's lover returns so cheerfully, nor the time-heavy domestic world of the woman. How nice if Philosophy should be wrong. But give her only ten years to prove her law, the poet says:

> O dear Sir, stumbling down the street,
> Continue, till you come to wars and wounds;
> Beat the air, Madam, till your house-clock sounds;
> And if no Lethe flows beneath your casement,
> And when ten years have not brought full effacement,
> Philosophy was wrong, and you may meet.

It is at "Blue Girls" that I would like to look closely. A man addresses, in thought, the girls of a seminary as in their blue uniforms they cross their campus.[12] "Practice your beauty, blue girls," he says (blue is the magical color in Ransom, the color of the good). But the tone is not quite that of the traditional *carpe diem*. It would be a rare group of modern college girls that would need anyone's urging to neglect the things of the mind and live for the present, and the man in the poem seems to know this well enough. Go ahead, then, and ignore your teachers, he says—perhaps he is one of them—

> Go listen to your teachers old and contrary
> Without believing a word.

> Tie the white fillets then about your hair
> And think no more of what will come to pass
> Than bluebirds that go walking on the grass
> And chattering on the air.

Go ahead and do what is as natural to you anyway as the chattering of the bluebirds. We can imagine the smallest amount of irony in his tone (especially if he is one of their teachers). It is the tone of an understanding that has passed at some point beyond exasperation. Ransom developed this tone, incidentally, from the first four stanzas of the *Fugitive* version, where it had still been mixed with the exasperation:

> And it is for this, God help us all for fools,
> You practice in the schools.

12. The girls are generally assumed to belong to the former Ward-Belmont College in Nashville, near which Ransom had an apartment.

After hitting that heavy a note, Ransom had had difficulty in the first version in asserting his *carpe diem* theme, saved for the final stanza.[13]

That is the tone, then, in which the *carpe diem* would be spoken to the modern American girls on their campuses; "would be" because the man addresses his words not to them, but to himself: "I *could* tell you a story which is true." What he *will* do is

> cry with my loud lips and publish
> Beauty which all our power shall never establish,
> It is so frail.

And the "loud lips" are at a further remove from Waller and Marvell. For beauty is the problem, rather than seduction; and the speaker, properly modest before his subject—perhaps he is also a poet—would have the girls understand the value of what they practice as unthinkingly as bluebirds. He would have them understand that in fact it is its very frailty that gives beauty its value.

The best moments of life are the poignant and clinging ones which are most informed of the fact of death; life is being rescued by death from what would have been its pure indifference, void of history and of drama, a mode of action which would be unconscious, physiological, mechanical. Would not goodness itself be meaningless, be just nothing at all, if goodness prevailed universally and did not have to reckon with the fact of evil? Death is the curse which time brings, but if it is not valuable in itself it is the cause of whatever else is of value. Without it our good moments could never be exalted and kept in memory, nor could the poet set them up in that handsome though specious "immortality" which is said to be within the power of his magic. This is the classical wisdom of poets.[14]

However, the poem does not end here. Like a good teacher the man has an example ready—the story he "*could* tell"—of

13. See appendix.
14. Ransom, "On Theodore Roethke's 'In a Dark Time,' " *The Contemporary Poet as Artist and Critic: Eight Symposia*, ed. Anthony Ostroff (Boston: Little, Brown, 1964), p. 30.

the failure of beauty and love. He knows

> a lady with a terrible tongue,
> Blear eyes fallen from blue,
> All her perfections tarnished—yet it is not long
> Since she was lovelier than any of you.

Do not become too proud, he thinks: a lady I know that you would think utterly different from yourselves, a native of that foreign country Age, was once a blue girl too. More interesting though is that these lines shift attention to the man himself, whose experience at this moment is complex. He experiences pleasure in watching the girls—pleasure expressed, for example, in the lovely line "Tie the white fillets then about your hair"— but pleasure that is qualified as we have seen by a little gentle irony, by a kind of fatherly, or pedagogical, objectivity, and that we now see is both mixed with the pain of contrast and heightened by the contrast. Possibly he must live with the lady of terrible tongue. At the same time he is faithful at least to the memory of what the lady once was, and proud of the memory, though he can joke to himself a little about the present: "Blear eyes fallen from blue." It is a complex response because it is an honest response made with full knowledge. With full knowledge he can still say, without bitterness—unlike the lady of terrible tongue?—practice your beauty.

The comparison of the blue girls to birds is a frequent kind of comparison with Ransom. Most often the bird is a dove; the lady of "In Process of a Noble Alliance" is a dove caught in a springe, and the poems that have to do with women and girls in *Two Gentlemen in Bonds* are printed under the subtitle "The Innocent Doves": "Vision by Sweetwater," "Eclogue," "Piazza Piece," "Blue Girls," "Hilda," "Janet Waking," "Lady Lost," and others. The little bird that is the "lady lost" clearly represents womankind, her description shading with a felicity of phrase from the avian into the human, and the moral is clear:

> "Let the owner come and claim possession,
> No questions will be asked. But stroke her gently
> With loving words, and she will evidently
> Return to her full soft-haired white-breasted fashion
> And her right home and her right passion."

These bird metaphors, except when they have a delicate rightness as in "Blue Girls" and "Vision by Sweetwater," may seem
merely sweet and quaint, an example of the chivalry which the
Southern men of another generation are supposed to have borne
toward their ladies. But Ransom looks at womankind from a
very different angle, which might be called the frontier Southern
attitude, in "Judith of Bethulia," where she emerges as dangerous and evil—a leopard.

"Judith of Bethulia" retells the story of the Apocryphal Book
of Judith but with several changes. The young widow of the
Apocrypha, who before her adventure had attracted little attention in her widow's garments, Ransom changes to a maiden who
"had not yet chosen her great captain or prince / Depositary
to her flesh," so that she seems the more powerfully attractive
to the young men "desperate to study / The invincible emanations of her white body." Whereas Judith in the Apocrypha ac-
complishes her mission to Holofernes's tent without any kind
of compromise to herself, Holofernes falling into a drunken sleep
almost the moment they are alone, in the poem she loosens "one
veil and another"—a description bound to suggest Salome—
"standing unafraid." And in the Apocrypha the only mention
made of Holofernes's head, after Judith returns with it in a bag,
is that it is hung up as an emblem to rally the Jews against
the enemy. In the poem:

> And the chieftain's head, with grinning sockets, and
>   varnished—
> Is it hung on the sky with a hideous epitaphy?
> No, the woman keeps the trophy.

This is quite a woman. Yet after her adventure her desirability
is even greater—for this Ransom found a hint in the book: "And
many desired her, but none knew her all the days of her life,

after that Manasses her husband was dead." What interests him most in the story, however, is the idea of the power the woman may have over the man. The death of Holofernes he describes as utterly ignominious: "she found his destruction easy," "she accomplished his derision"; and the young men, since their oppressor was also a fellow male and a warrior, feel fear as strong as their desire:

> It is stated she went reluctant to that orgy,
> Yet madness fevers our young men, and not the clergy
> Nor the elders have turned them unto modesty since.
> Inflamed by the thought of her naked beauty with desire?
> Yes, and chilled with fear and despair.

Judith is woman considered, not as an "innocent dove," but as the daughter of Eve.

It is a distinctive poem—the best-known of Ransom's poems, according to an English critic, speaking presumably for Ransom's English audience. Each stanza concludes with a question and an answer, the answer making up the final line, which is short by two stresses. Beginning with stanza two the questions are asked by the old men who are the narrator's audience, and to them Ransom gives in his recorded reading a tone of foolish incredulity: "Nor brushed her with even so much as a daisy?" The narrator's brief answer, by contrast, he sounds in the driest of tones: "She found his destruction easy." And the shortness of the line that concludes the poem contributes to the flatness and the hopeless finality of the tone: "Yes, and chilled with fear and despair." But the first line of the poem is the striking line: "Beautiful as the flying legend of some leopard." It is common to say that rumors fly, but a legend we think of as "growing up"—more like a tree than a bird. Therefore *flying* seems to attach itself to *leopard* as much as to *legend*. A flying leopard might be one with an unbelievable leap, or one that made a large area of the land his domain, showing up at impossible distances. But granted that a legend may fly, what kind of legend about a leopard would it likely be? (Ransom apparently has no particular legend in mind.) Perhaps a legend about a bold and powerful animal that has terrorized the villages. Would such a legend be "beautiful"? Like *flying,* the word *beautiful* I think attaches itself also to leopard. However it is gotten, the effect is a sense of a fabulous creature—the leopard Judith, beautiful, evil.

In "Vision by Sweetwater," "The Tall Girl," and "First Travels of Max," innocence is confronted with evil not through knowledge of death (death in Ransom's poems is an agency of evil, and the value it gives to life is the most important way that evil defines the good), but is confronted with evil directly, supernaturally. The best of these poems by far—one of the best of all of Ransom's poems, in fact—is "Vision by Sweetwater." Randall Jarrell regretted its exclusion from the 1945 *Selected Poems* as the only mistake of taste Ransom made in the volume, and Ransom has included it in his revised edition. Here is its bird metaphor:

> Robin's sisters and my Aunt's lily daughter
> Laughed and talked, and tinkled light as wrens
> If there were a little colony all hens
> To go walking by the steep turn of Sweetwater.

The lines that enter the most private level of a reader's memory—the level that the mind touches at unliterary moments and with little effort of the will, as when one is driving a car, or floating in a quarry with his chin on a log as Jarrell said he was doing when he discovered that he knew Frost's "Provide Provide" by heart—these lines may get there mainly because of the imagery in one instance—Yeats's beast slouching towards Bethlehem—or because of the meter in another—

> The witch that came (the withered hag)
> To wash the steps with pail and rag
> Was once the beauty Abishag . . .
>   ("Provide Provide")

Of course other departments of the verse must be functioning at the same time, and accordingly Ransom's lines sketch a pretty picture and sound their vowels agreeably: "walking by the steep turn of Sweetwater." But most often in Ransom it is, I think,

the phrasing, the graceful relaxation of the syntax. The lines
proceed toward their goal a little more leisurely than a short,
"efficient" poem ought to permit—it is "texture" half ignoring
"structure"—as in the third and fourth lines above, which add
nothing to an unremarkable though appropriate metaphor, add
only a little to the picture, but are a pleasure.

The moment described is perfect: the girls stepping along
lovely and innocent, nature co-operative—"The willows, clouds,
deep meadowgrass, and the river"—a long summer afternoon's
visit at Sweetwater (the sort of name the fathers have given
to spots where Nature seems especially benevolent) stretching
ahead.[15] But the narrator, a child then, watching his cousin and
her friends sweeping along in their long dresses, sees suddenly
something Greek in their aspect potential of tragedy, and hears
from the future a sound of terror:

> Let them alone, dear Aunt, just for one minute
> Till I go fishing in the dark of my mind:
> Where have I seen before, against the wind,
> These bright virgins, robed and bare of bonnet,
>
> Flowing with music of their strange quick tongue
> And adventuring with delicate paces by the stream,—
> Myself a child, old suddenly at the scream
> From one of the white throats which it hid among?

Where does the child get his sudden insight? The implication,
psychologically, is of the collective unconscious: "the dark"
of the mind; theologically, of original sin.

"First Travels of Max" treats a child's vision of evil quite
differently—though there is implied again the doctrine of original sin—and with far less success. Disobeying his elders, Max
walks into "Fool's Forest," where

> The only innocent thing in there was Max,
> And even he had cursed his little sisters.

15. One assumes naturally that Sweetwater is a Tennessee place-name, but
Ransom has said that it is near his wife's home in Colorado, where he got
the idea for the poem (Vanderbilt Literary Symposium, April, 1960).

As he "half expected," he meets the "Red Witch" herself. At
the end of the poem, on his return home, there is a little irony
in the disparity between his knowledge and his still-innocent
appearance, with "his famous curls unsmoothed"; but it seems
a small irony for so long a poem. In it there is not the easy
grace of phrasing of "Vision by Sweetwater," but the looseness
and the rambling whimsicality of the middle stanzas of "Puncture." And the tone that results from a dry adult treatment
of fairy tale materials becomes tiresome, especially where the
tone is conveyed through the three- or four-word sentences:

> "Littlest and last Van Vrooman, do you come too?"
> She knew him, it appeared, would know him better,
> The scarlet hulk of hell with a fat bosom
> Pirouetting at the bottom of the forest.
> Certainly Max had come. But he was going;
> Unequal contests never being commanded
> On young knights only armed in innocency.
> "When I am a grown man I will come here
> And cut your head off!" That was very well.
> Not a true heart beating in Christendom
> Could have said more, but that for the present would do.

A more likely look of evil than the witch's is that of the
Queens of Hell in the sonnet "The Tall Girl." They have "lissome necks to crane," betraying their association with the Antichrist of "Armageddon," who plays a "lissome flute"; whereas
the Queen of Heaven, appropriately outnumbered, appears "in
the likeness, I hear, of a plain motherly woman." Furthermore,
the Queens of Hell are the much more persuasive speakers, dis-
armingly offhand:

> "If the young miss with gold hair might not disdain,
> We would esteem her company over the plain,
> To profit us all where the dogs will be out barking,
> And we'll go by the windows where the young men are
>   working,
> And tomorrow we will all come home again."

The last line is cunning. It is their assurance that the tall girl
can come home again, that she and her world will be exactly
as before. It is the serpent's assurance to Eve that she can taste

the fruit without committing herself to time or to the chain reaction of cause-and-effect: "Ye shall not surely die." Taste without commitment, says the serpent to Eve; commitment without responsibility, says the serpent to the Determinist; responsibility without consequence, says the serpent to the Existentialist. It is the Queen of Heaven's disadvantage that, very like a mother, she can say little more than *no*: "This never will come to good!" And she confesses the limit of her power when she adds in the final line, from "the other side of the road": "Just an old woman, my pet, that wishes you well."[16]

The subject of "Two in August" and "Parting, without a Sequel" is the end of love, which comes abruptly and a little mysteriously.

> How sleepers groan, twitch, wake to such a mood
> Is not well understood,
> Nor why two entities grown almost one
> Should rend and murder trying to get undone,
> With individual tigers in their blood.

These are the husband and wife who wake on an August night to an argument that terrifies and bewilders them with its intensity. As she paces the floor, time becomes oppressive in her consciousness. Is what is happening inevitable in time?

> She in terror fled from the marriage chamber
> Circuiting the dark rooms like a string of amber
> Round and round and back,
> And would not light one lamp against the black,
> And heard the clock that clanged: Remember, Remember.

He paces barefooted out into the yard:

> High in the trees the night-mastered birds were crying
> With fear upon their tongues, no singing nor flying
> Which are their lovely attitudes by dawn.

> Whether those bird-cries were of heaven or hell
> There is no way to tell.

16. Why "the *tall* girl"? Tallness has for Ransom somewhat the same magical properties as blueness. In "Tom, Tom the Piper's Son" (now revised as "The Vanity of the Bright Young Men"), one of the signs of Tom's self-absorption is that he is "tricked by white birds or tall women to no wonder."

Clearly we are meant to answer: hell. It is the answer given us also by the two serpent metaphors in "Parting, without a Sequel." A girl has declared the end to a long relationship in a letter "with characters venomous and hatefully curved"; even while hoping that it might be lost somewhere, she gives it to a messenger:

> Away went the messenger's bicycle,
> His serpent's track went up the hill forever.

"Forever": she too is oppressed by the thought of time, "observing" in her act "the ruin of her younger years." And she stands and watches

> Under her father's vaunting oak
> Who kept his peace in wind and sun, and glistened
> Stoical in the rain; to whom she listened
> If he spoke.
>
> And now the agitation of the rain
> Rasped his sere leaves, and he talked low and gentle
> Reproaching the wan daughter by the lintel;
> Ceasing and beginning again.

The great oak of her father, the coming and going of the wind in it, a certain Biblical flavor in the phrase "the wan daughter by the lintel," cast the mind backward, and give her act the intenser sadness of a history old as the Garden.

Jane Sneed and John Black thresh the matter out in "Eclogue," the longest poem—eighty-five lines—in *Selected Poems,* and a poem of high quality throughout. They are former childhood friends who later became lovers for a time, and now in their puzzled and disillusioned maturity they discuss their former selves. In their dialogue the connection between the fact of mortality and the idea of evil is explicit. "Time involved us; in his toils / We learned to fear," says John Black.

> And every day since then
> We are mortals teasing for immortal spoils,
> Desperate women and men.

JANE SNEED CONSENTED: It was nothing but this.
Love suffereth long, is kind—but not in fear.
For boys run banded, and simple sweethearts kiss,
Till in one day the dream of Death appear—
Then metamorphosis.

JOHN BLACK SAID: To explain mistrust and wars,
Theogony has a black witch with hell's broth;
Or a preposterous marriage of fleshless stars;
Or the Fiend's own naked person; or God wroth
Fingering his red scars.

And philosophy, an art of equal worth,
Tells of a flaw in the firmament—spots in the sun—
A Third Day's error when the upheaving earth
Was young and prime—a Fate reposed upon
The born before their birth.

JANE SNEED WITH GRIM LIPS MOCKED HIM: Who
    can tell—
Not I, not you—about those mysteries!
Something, John Black, came flapping out of hell
And wrought between us, and the chasm is
Digged, and it digged it well.

Yet Jane Sneed has a shy hope. The fact that she can at least
imagine happiness should, she thinks, be of some significance.

I suppose it stands
Just so. Yet I can picture happiness—
Perhaps there wander lovers in some lands
Who when Night comes, when it is fathomless,
Consort their little hands;

And well, John Black, the darkened lovers may,
The hands hold much of heat in little storage,
The eyes are almost torches good as day,
And one flame to the other flame cries Courage,
When heart to heart slide they;

So they keep unafraid the whole night through,
Till the sun of a sudden glowing through the bushes
They wake and laugh, their eyes again are blue,
And listen! are those not the doves, the thrushes?
Look there! the golden dew.

I would like, by the way, to state a preference for an earlier version of those last two lines:

> They run to the fields, and beautiful the thrushes,
> Fabulous the dew.

I find more joy and energy in the simple "they run" than in "listen!" and "Look there!" which seem overdone.

John Black has the "last say":

> O innocent dove,
> This is a dream. We lovers mournfully
> Exchange our bleak despairs. We are one part love
> And nine parts bitter thought. As well might be
> Beneath ground as above.

However, if we know Ransom we will not take John Black's word as conclusive. Jane Sneed's dream contains Ransom's usual images of hope and life: the blue eyes, the birds; and in the tentativeness of its hope—"*Perhaps* there wander lovers in *some* lands"—it resembles the ending of another poem, "Somewhere Is Such a Kingdom."

"Somewhere Is Such a Kingdom" is one of Ransom's most charming poems. It is written in couplets of varying lengths, mostly of four stresses but also of three and even two; among the fours are some perfectly regular octosyllabics sounding their pleasant little music, as in Marvell, between the prosy rhythms usual with Ransom.

The speaker of the poem takes refuge, for a while at least, in the sounds of the birds for the images they bring of an ideally civilized life. A grace something like the Renaissance ideal of *sprezzatura:*

> The famous kingdom of the birds
> Has a sweet tongue and liquid words,
> The red-birds polish their notes
> In their easy practised throats.
> Smooth as orators are the thrushes
> Of the airy city of the bushes.

Or a healthy sexuality (the lines take one back to Chaucer's Chanticleer):

> And God reward the fierce cock wrens
> Who have such suavity with their hens.

Or a contented home life:

> To me this has its worth
> As I sit upon the earth
> Lacking my winter and quiet hearth.
> For I go up into a nook
> With a mind burdened or a book,
> And hear no strife nor quarreling
> As the birds and their wives sing.

For to this man, too, evil has manifested itself apparently in some domestic disturbance, rather than in one of the large issues of courts and nations. "I suppose it's not been disputed," Ransom has said in speaking of his poetry, "that the domestic situation is by long odds the most important of all the human situations. Domestic problems must be solved if a man is going to be successful."[17]

The man cannot be certain that the lives of the birds are as idyllic as, by contrast, they seem at the moment. If evil does exist among them, he knows from his own experience what it must be like:

> Girls that have unlawful dreams
> Will waken full of their own screams,
> And boys that get too arrant
> Will have rows with a parent,—
> And when friend falls out with friend
> All songs must have quick end.

But though he finally decides that the bird kingdom must be very like the human—"Have not these gentlemen wives?"—he is stubborn:

17. *Conversations* . . . , p. 19.

But when they croak and fleer and swear,
My dull heart I must take elsewhere;
For I will see if God has made
Otherwhere another shade
Where the men or beasts or birds
Exchange few words and pleasant words.
And dare I think it is absurd
If no such beast were, no such bird?

His hope could not be more sidling in its expression: "dare I think it is absurd?" There is a connotation to *kingdom,* in the title, and to *shade* that suggests such a country may be found, if at all, only the other side of the grave. Nevertheless, his secret mind like Jane Sneed's remains pointed in its direction, irrationally against the grain of his experience; as a line of Robert Penn Warren states it, "Grace undreamed is grace foregone."

The belief in the *possibility* of hope is the conclusion also of "Persistent Explorer." The explorer, however, is not fleeing an evil world, but a world in which neither good nor evil is possible: a world of mere fact, bare of cause either to "cower or rejoice." *God Without Thunder* contains a passage apropos:

The common fate of an impersonal object, when thrown upon our tender mercies, is to receive a term, to enter through the term into our routine experience, and to be disqualified. But we may recover the sense of the object ordinarily, if we will boldly personify it, or attribute to it the dignity of a person. . . . In the modern style, dryads, oreads, and nymphs have gone nearly out of use. In our period things have suffered the extreme of humiliation, and come to be generally disesteemed as simply *the objects for our sciences to possess and for ourselves to use.* The demonic terms have largely disappeared. . . . The personal terms nevertheless persist unquestionably in our thinking. They are those personifications of things that have been condemned under what has been called the "pathetic fallacy": for example, a breath of wind; the laughing waters. . . . Objects thus evoked are perfect ghosts, with a fabulous investment of substantial quality.[18]

18. Pp. 290–291.

As the explorer at the beginning of the poem climbs toward a waterfall, his "literal ears" are "teased" by its roar, and he is on the brink of the largest kind of experience.

> But listen as he might, look fast or slow,
> It was water, only water, tons of it
> Dropping into the gorge, and every bit
> Was water—the insipid chemical H_2O.
>
> Its thunder smote him somewhat as the loud
> Words of the god that rang around a man
> Walking by the Mediterranean.
> Its cloud of froth was whiter than the cloud
>
> That clothed the goddess sliding down the air
> Unto a mountain shepherd, white as she
> That issued from the smoke refulgently.
> The cloud was, but the goddess was not there.
>   .   .   .   .   .   .
> And if the smoke and rattle of water drew
>
> From the deep thickets of his mind the train,
> The fierce fauns and the timid tenants there,
> That burst their bonds and rushed upon the air,
> Why, he must turn and beat them down again.

The phrase "the deep thickets of his mind" provides a farther-reaching source for the fauns than Bulfinch: it is the cultural memory from which comes the boy's Sophoclean vision at Sweetwater. Why, then, if these deities should magically re-emerge, would he "beat them down again"? I think the reason must be their anachronism, and their foreignness to this scene; the same idea is expressed in the poem "Philomela": "Never was she baptized." What train of deities the explorer *would* welcome, he does not know; he only knows his need of them:

> Furious the spectacle
> But it spelled nothing, there was not any spell
> Bidding him whether cower or rejoice.
>
> What would he have it spell? He scarcely knew;
> Only that water and nothing but water filled
> His eyes and ears, nothing but water that spilled.

However, he makes no "unreasonable outcry," he has the Ransom stoicism. After all, "there were many ways of living," the final stanza begins,

> And let his enemies gibe, but let them say
> That he would throw this continent away
> And seek another country,—as he would do.

Continent and *country* are large words—standing, of course, for the geography of the soul, as in "Eclogue" and "Somewhere Is Such a Kingdom." But Ransom, typically, tones down the effect by the thought of the gibing enemies, which goes with the "rueful grin" on the explorer's face; and by the offhand tone of the final clause, "as he would do." No heroes or prophets speak in these poems, only the quietly hopeful.

Even Prometheus in Ransom's poem about him is not *bound*, only hemmed in: "Prometheus in Straits." His punishment is disillusion:

> Though I be Prometheus my mind may have wandered
> To bring my pious offices to this people.

Although the poem is slight, it does contain this humorous stanza:

> To the colleges then and the modern masterpieces?
> Not now though I risk the damage of your inference;
> Before your explications respect ceases
> For the centers lost in so absurd circumference;
> You have only betrayed them by your exegesis
> And provoke me to gestures not of deference.

"Prometheus in Straits," "Persistent Explorer," "Old Mansion," and "Philomela" consider time historically rather than metaphysically, stating or implying a contrast between the present and the past; and these, with "Man without Sense of Direction," must be the poems the critics have uppermost in mind who have said that the dissociation of sensibility is Ransom's major theme, although Robert Penn Warren, who first applied the term, and Cleanth Brooks have sometimes meant by it a psychological dissociation—that is, a dualism of thought

and feeling in man's nature—rather than the historical dissociation that Eliot meant. They are ambiguous here. Warren seems
to mean a psychological dissociation when he defines its two
aspects in Ransom's verse: "Man is a creature little lower than
the angels and, at the same time, of the brute creation; again,
there is a conflict between the scientific vision of quantity and
that vision concerned with quality. The issue in itself is as old
as man."[19] He means an historical dissociation when he says
that the center of the verse "is to be defined in terms of that
sensibility whose decay Ransom, along with various other critics,
has bewailed. . . . To an astonishing degree, in far more than
a majority of cases, the hero or heroine of the poem is a sufferer
from that complaint of 'dissociation of sensibility.' " However,
in the same essay he distinguishes between the "historical"
method of Eliot's irony and the "psychological" method of Ransom's.[20] As for an historical dissociation, Ransom believes there
is no such thing, because there was no *association* to begin with,
at least not in the historical past.

Lamenting the modern dualism of thought and feeling, Eliot thinks
he finds it bridged in the older order of English poetry, though the
technique by which it was accomplished was let go, and has never
been rediscovered.
I confess that I know very little about that; and I must add that,
having worked to the best of my ability to find the thing Eliot refers
to in the 17th Century poets, and failed, I incline to think there
was nothing of the kind there. . . . We must not like some philosophers become the fools of the shining but impractical ideal of "unity"
or of "fusion." The aspiration here is for some sort of fusion of two
experiences that ordinarily repel one another: the abstracted exercise
of reason in hard fact and calculation; and the inclusive experience
of literally everything at once. . . . It would seem that from that
precise moment when the race discovers that what has seemed to
be an undifferentiated unity is really a complex of specialized func-
tions, there can be no undifferentiated unity again; no return. We
do not quite know how to feel a thought. The best we can do is

19. "A Note on Three Southern Poets," *Poetry*, XL, No. 2 (May, 1932),
110.
20. "John Crowe Ransom: A Study in Irony," *The Virginia Quarterly Review*,
XI, No. 1 (Jan., 1935), 103, 110.

to conduct a thought without denying all the innocent or irrelevant feelings in the process. The dualism remains.[21]

The theme of "Old Mansion" is the contrast between a past imaged in a crumbling Southern mansion, and the present, represented by a curious but condescending passer-by who requests a look inside the house and is turned away.

> on retreating I saw myself in the token,
> How loving from my dying weed the feather curled
> On the languid air; and I went with courage shaken
> To dip, alas, into some unseemlier world.

This point is reached, however, only after ten quatrains that keep up, sometimes tediously, a single minor tone of irony directed by the speaker at both himself and the mansion. The irony is not a means of coming to terms with an emotion; there is not much emotion to begin with, and only the one bare thought, about the unseemlier present, at the end of the poem. Yet there is, as usual, a good deal of verbal skill in its pentameter quatrain. This seems to be the stanza that Ransom has felt the most comfortable in: about one-quarter of the selected poems are written in it. Built most frequently of a single sentence, it is a convenient length for the complexly mannered statement. I suspect that it was in this stanza that the younger Fugitives were most often tempted to imitate Ransom. Tate once mistook Ransom as the author of one of Davidson's poems in this stanza.

The man without sense of direction, in the poem of that title, would seem to be a classical case of the historical dissociation of sensibility. But in fact the poem offers no diagnosis of any kind:

> The larks' tongues are never stilled
> Where the pale spread straw of sunlight lies
> Then what invidious gods have willed
> Him to be seized so otherwise?

There is nothing peculiarly modern about the stage on which he suffers; rather than urban and sordid as in Eliot, the setting

---

21. *The New Criticism*, pp. 183–184.

is almost sappily rustic:

> Birds of the field and beasts of the stable
> Are swollen with rapture and make uncouth
> Demonstration of joy, which is a babble
> Offending the ear of the fervorless youth.

There is no contrast between his time and an earlier, no indication that his disease, like snow over Ireland, is general. Though Ransom may leave it to the reader to say for himself how general the disease is, there is no generalization in the poem itself. The man is merely a single "creature,"

> Of noblest mind and powerful leg
> Who cannot fathom nor perform his nature.

At points the man's plight is tragi-comic: "He flails his arms, he moves his lips"; and when a more somber tone is sounded, it is as much on his young wife's behalf as on his:

> So he stands muttering; and rushes
> Back to the tender thing in his charge
> With clamoring tongue and taste of ashes
> And a small passion to feign large.

> But let his cold lips be her omen,
> She shall not kiss that harried one
> To peace, as men are served by women
> Who comfort them in darkness and in sun.

His inability to love his wife is the poem's focus, and the interconnection of love with other experiences is the poem's theme. Because he has no direction—"cause, time, nor country"—he cannot love. And because he cannot love, he has no direction. How he got into the circle, who can tell, and who can tell how he may get out again? The way out would have to be as mysterious and as personal as the way in. What he is "without" is unteachable: the simple trick of day-to-day living, of performing "his nature." He is like Ibsen's Hedda Gabler, who dies in the same weary circle.

A word on the poem's meter: its quatrain is meant apparently to have four stresses to the line, instead of the usual five, though it is difficult in some lines to suppress a fifth primary stress; but the number of syllables ranges from seven to thirteen. Ransom has commented on this practice in discussing "Bells for John Whiteside's Daughter":

I would call it, perhaps, accentual meter; that is to say, we just count the number of accented or stressed syllables in the line and let the unstressed syllables take care of themselves. So that sometimes you get two stresses coming together, and sometimes you run over two or three, or maybe even four, unstressed syllables at once—which was against the rule of the old poets—but the moderns have done that a good deal.[22]

What results, though obviously not strict iambic, is not quite anapaestic either, as we can see in the stanza which contains the largest number of unstressed syllables:

> Wheth er by street, or in field full of hon ey,
> At tend ed by clouds of the crea tures of air
> Or shoul der ing the ci ty's com pan ion ing ma ny,
> His doom is on him; and how can he care

"Philomela" also is written in this somewhat prosy meter; and appropriately, for the American says that he has no ear:

> My ears are called capacious but they failed me,
> Her classics registered a little flat!

"My scene is prose," he says in an earlier version, despairing that he may ever appreciate European culture, of which Philomela's song is the symbol. However, much of the poem's irony is directed at the classical and Anglo-European tradition as well. The direction of the irony is clear in the following stanza, beginning with the mock gravity of "pernoctated":

> I pernoctated with the Oxford students once,
> And in the quadrangles, in the cloisters, on the Cher,
> Precociously knocked at antique doors ajar,
> Fatuously touched the hems of the hierophants,
> Sick of my dissonance.

22. *Conversations* . . . , p. 22.

It is the two-way irony, directed at self and at object, that we find in "Old Mansion," but more broad and humorous. Does it have a point, or is it no more than the irony, frequent among contemporary writers, that will not leave room for a right answer, only for the mysterious rightness of the writer?—If you cannot get the English tone, you are lost, and if you try you are insecure.

The point lies not in the value of the tradition itself, but in the impossibility of importing it entire to another continent.

> At Fontainebleau it may be the bird was gallicized;
> Never was she baptized.

Hers is an "untranslatable refrain," a "delicate dirge" that cannot "run democratic." The doubleness of the irony derives from the American's dilemma: his need to belong not merely to a society, but to a culture; his natural dissatisfaction with the only truly rich cultural experience available to him: "I rose, and venomously spat." For it is not his native experience, even if he were not handicapped anyway by a dialectical-scientific bias of mind, which makes of Philomela's legend an "improbable tale." And he must doubt whether a native experience may ever be possible "in a boundless cloudless public place"—a modern democracy—among "an inordinate race." The dilemma is part of the larger dilemma Ransom defines in his epilogue to *God Without Thunder*:

For better or worse, a man is a member of his own race, or his own tribe. He will have to prosper or suffer as it prospers or suffers. The religion that he requires must have the character of being his own social institution. If there is not a religious institution that suits him quite near at home, he will have to go without one.

. . . . . .

Why not bid the West go Anglican, or Episcopal? . . . I am an Anglophile, and I wish my country might be more so. But I am not so Anglophile as I am American. And I find myself sometimes, as I find my neighbor more frequently, abhorring Anglicanism and Episcopacy. For reasons perhaps that are social and political, and inarticulate but deep—for inherited reasons. Therefore I propose no such thing. I still seek the religion that will be the expression of the social solidarity of my own community.

There is Presbyterianism; and Methodism; and Baptistry; there are plenty of other sectarian possibilities. These bodies are evidently close to the genius of my kind of community. But they have declined rather far from orthodoxy, as I see it—and as what Western religious body has not? They secularize themselves more and more every day. It is hard to give them an endorsement.

.   .   .   .   .   .

Under these circumstances it will be a bolder man than I who has an extremely specific or concrete proposal to offer to the Western cis-Atlantic world seeking its religious expression.[23]

It may be objected that I am making the poem sound much more serious than it is. But the humorous tone does not carry into the concluding lines; these, addressed to Philomela, are pure in their tone of regret:

> Unto more beautiful, persistently more young,
> Thy fabulous provinces belong.

There is a story of a professor, a teacher, and colleague of the Fugitives, whose method of teaching poetry was to read a poem aloud to his class, gaze out the window a moment and say "Isn't that beautiful?" and then turn back to his book and read another poem. One hesitates to say much more about "Captain Carpenter" than—not "Isn't that beautiful?" certainly, but something equally enthusiastic, and brief. And not much more has been said about it, though it is one of Ransom's best known poems. "I don't know whether it means anything beyond what it says," Ransom himself has said.

There's an old hero who dies with his boots on, so to speak, and I've been asked if he could not have represented the Old South. Or if he could not have stood for the old-time religion. But those ideas did not enter my mind when I was composing the little ballad.[24]

We are supposed to be too sophisticated critically in these days to trust wholly what an author has to say about his own work,

23. Pp. 325–327.
24. "John Crowe Ransom Reads from His Own Works."

even if we are not put on our guard anyway by something like
the modesty that speaks of "the little ballad." If the Captain
does not stand for the Old South, at least there is a resemblance
between the manner of his defeat and that of the old families
in Faulkner, who lose because they will not compromise their
honor and stoop to the tactics of the Snopeses.

> Captain Carpenter mounted up one day
> And rode straightway into a stranger rogue
> That looked unchristian but be that as may
> The Captain did not wait upon prologue.
>
> But drew upon him out of his great heart
> The other swung against him with a club
> And cracked his two legs at the shinny part
> And let him roll and stick like any tub.

The Captain, who would engage the enemy in honorable fashion,
is defeated by a caveman-like club. Or if the Captain is not
to be associated with any religious point-of-view, there *are* these
facts: that his foes include a "rogue / That looked unchristian,"
"the wife of Satan," and "a black devil"; that he rides forth
"in hell's despite"; and that his name, Carpenter, in this context
sounds suspiciously like a symbol.

But neither interpretation would account for the whole poem.
It is enough to say that this is a good man, that he lives by
a high code—and that his career, he being utterly innocent in
reckoning the odds he is up against in Ransom's dualistic world,
is as comic as it is violent. He has already been ignominiously
"twined" of his nose and had his legs cracked "at the shinny
part" when he comes upon the wife of Satan.

> Their strokes and counters whistled in the wind
> I wish he had delivered half his blows

(a tone of amused pity for the hero who cannot hit his target)

> But where she should have made off like a hind

(as in the story books)

> The bitch bit off his arms at the elbows.

The wound would seem somehow more heroic if she had taken

the whole arm while she was at it. After this loss and the subsequent loss of ears and eyes, he is still heard asking quixotically
"in the grimmest tone / If any enemy yet there was to fight?"

However, the poet does make the Captain one of his blue-eyed.
Despite the Captain's absurdity, he is at least superior to his
vanquishers, on whom the poet invokes the profoundest curses.
Especially is he contrasted in his courage and manliness with
his last foe, the "neatest knave that ever was seen / Stepping
in perfume from his lady's bower." The fop is a curious figure,
and the only one of the good man's enemies who is not Evil
incarnate. I think that he is meant to show a peculiarly modern
character: "the sleek upstart," the poet calls him. He is ruthless,
efficient, irreverent. He gets what he wants with a minimum
of time and effort, and with one eye out for appearances, for
public relations—"With gentle apology and touch refined":

> The rogue in scarlet and grey soon knew his mind
> He wished to get his trophy and depart
> With gentle apology and touch refined
> He pierced him and produced the Captain's heart.

"Pierced" and "produced": it sounds more like an operation
than a killing; nothing personal, the fop might say. We almost
forget that it is the very heart of Captain Carpenter he is appro-
priating, the seat of the soul. Not content with defeating the
Captain, with knocking "old fellows in the dust," he violates
him; and the final curse is reserved for him alone. But the curse
is delivered in the tone of the rest of the poem:

> The curse of hell upon the sleek upstart
> That got the Captain finally on his back
> And took the red red vitals of his heart
> And made the kites to whet their beaks clack clack.

The "clack clack" humorously recalls the world of Mother Goose.
The apparently comic and the possibly serious, that we can talk
about only in separation, are mixed in the poem as one
experience.

Let us grant that the poem may not mean "anything beyond
what it says"; that is, that Ransom simply sat down in a spirit

of irresponsible fun and said to himself that he would try writing a broadside ballad—that it is even a piece of automatic writing. And what an accomplished verbalist it shows him to be. But whatever his first impulse, he could not help being John Crowe Ransom. So his values would quite naturally have gotten into the poem and, this being Ransom, the near-negation of those values in humor and irony.

It is of "Antique Harvesters" that Ransom says, "This is my Southern poem."[25] The *Southwest Review*, which first printed the poem, quoted the poet as writing that it is "the appeal of the Old South to the young men to stand by the cause," and it gives "the viewpoint of the local lean old veterans."[26] By the latter he seems to mean carefully to distinguish the poem's viewpoint from his own, for the poem has a peculiarly weary tone for an appeal (the fact, though, that he chose this viewpoint should be of some significance). It is, in fact, an appeal that admits in the same breath the probability that the cause is at an end. Compare it to Davidson's "Randall, My Son":

> And tell me then, will you some day bequeath
> To your own son not born or yet begotten,
> The lustre of a sword that sticks in sheath,
> A house that crumbles and a fence that's rotten?
> Take, what I leave, your own land unforgotten;
> Hear, what I hear, in a far chase new begun
> An old horn's husky music, Randall, my son.
>
> (*Lee in the Mountains*, p. 39)

When the point is reached in Ransom's poem for the call-to-arms, what comes is almost mincing: "Angry as wasp-music be your cry then"; an unheroic simile, certainly, a comparison of the type called "downward." And the verb is not in the imperative, but in the subjunctive.

The direct appeal to the young men, such as it is, comes only in the final three stanzas. Mostly the gaze of the old men is

25. *Ibid.*
26. "The Authors in this Issue," *Southwest Review*, X, No. 3 (April, 1925), 125.

upon themselves, as in the dignity of their history and the communion of ritual they endure for only a little longer on a declining land.

> Tawny are the leaves turned but they still hold,
> And it is harvest; what shall this land produce?
> A meager hill of kernels, a runnel of juice;
> Declension looks from our land, it is old.
> Therefore let us assemble, dry, grey, spare,
> And mild as yellow air.

They make the common joke of fathers upon their sons' foreignness to hard work: "Bare the arms, dainty youths, bend the knees." For the rest there is a feeling of distance between them and the young, and none of the conviction in Davidson's poem, which speaks of the "far chase new begun," that the future can be as vital as the past. Tense in Ransom's poem is future perfect:

> And by an autumn tone
> As by a grey, as by a green, you will have known
> Your famous Lady's image.

What is dominant is an atmosphere engagingly mellow, sad, a little hazy, in which nothing is really seen, composed of certain repeated colors: "tawny," "grey," "mild as yellow air," "full bronze," "autumn tone," "bronze burdens."

The irony in this poem is more than a kind of tempering: it works against any tone of appeal or resolution. This may be seen especially in the final stanza. Ransom has seemed uncertain about the stanza, leaving it out of the version printed in *Two Gentlemen in Bonds*, then restoring it in the 1945 *Selected Poems*. Without the stanza, the poem had this conclusion in *Two Gentlemen:*

> And if one say that easily will your hands
> More prosper in other lands,
>
> Angry as wasp-music be your cry then:
> "Forsake the Proud Lady, of the heart of fire,
> The look of snow, to the praise of a dwindled choir,
> Song of degenerate specters that were men?
> The sons of the fathers shall keep her, worthy of
> What these have done in love."

This version was printed in 1927, when Ransom and the other Fugitive-Agrarians were beginning to turn their attention to the future of the South. Though set to "wasp-music" rather than to trumpet and drum, it was definitely a more positive ending than the present one:

> True, it is said of our Lady, she ageth.
> But see, if you peep shrewdly, she hath not stooped;
> Take no thought of her servitors that have drooped,
> For we are nothing; and if one talk of death—
> Why, the ribs of the earth subsist frail as a breath
> If but God wearieth.

The diminutive quality of the verb *peep* tends to cancel any conviction there may be that "She hath not stooped," as does the teasing archaism of *ageth* and *hath*, with *wearieth* the only archaic words in the poem. Most significant, though, are the two lines that conclude: they change the subject in effect, by expanding the subject to include the metaphysical, which, as I have noted, is Ransom's natural element.[27]

The poems that I have been discussing in this chapter have all been reprinted in *Selected Poems*. There are, however, a number of out-of-print poems that deserve reading, and may even seem to some readers more interesting than a few of the selected poems. I have in mind two in *Chills and Fever*: "April Treason" and "Blackberry Winter."

The theme of "April Treason" is that of Thomas Mann's novelette "Tonio Kröger": the distinction between art and life, the conflict between the artist and the man. Ransom's brief narrative in fact suggests an episode in "Tonio Kröger," that in which the young writer is made too restless to work by the fine spring

27. An idea in his review of *Murder in the Cathedral* comes to mind: "A drama that starts religious, but reverts, declines, very distinctly towards snappiness. Can Eliot sustain the religious tone? As critic, as prose man, yes, for anybody can sustain any tone, by main strength; as poet, you do it only if the tone is you, or is grace of God implanted in you" (*The World's Body*, p. 166). It has been suggested that Ransom was an Agrarian by main strength.

weather and visits his painter friend Lisabeta with his complaint:

"Five minutes ago, not far from here, I met a man I know, Adalbert, the novelist. 'God damn the spring!' says he in the aggressive way he has. 'It is and always has been the most ghastly time of the year. Can you sit still and work out even the smallest effect when your blood tickles till it's positively indecent and you are teased by a whole host of irrelevant sensations that when you look at them turn out to be unworkable trash?'

. . . . . .

"Yes, it is true; spring is a bad time for work; and why? Because we are feeling too much. Nobody but a beginner imagines that he who creates must feel. . . . If you care too much about what you have to say, if your heart is too much in it, you can be pretty sure of making a mess. You get pathetic, you wax sentimental; something dull and doddering, without roots or outlines, with no sense of humour—something tiresome and banal grows under your hand, and you get nothing out of it but apathy in your audience and disappointment and misery in yourself. For so it is, Lisabeta; feeling, warm, heartfelt feeling, is always banal and futile; only the irritations and icy ecstasies of the artist's corrupted nervous system are artistic. The artist must be unhuman, extra-human; he must stand in a queer aloof relationship to our humanity; only so is he in a position, I ought to say only so would he be tempted, to represent it, to present it, to portray it to good effect. The very gift of style, of form and expression, is nothing else than this cool and fastidious attitude towards humanity; you might say there has to be this impoverishment and devastation as a preliminary condition. For sound natural feeling, say what you like, has no taste. It is all up with the artist as soon as he becomes a man and begins to feel.[28]

I have quoted at a little length because, except for Mann's suspicion of the artist as a human *manqué* ("the artist's corrupted nervous system . . . *queer* aloof relationship . . . only so would he be *tempted* . . ."), what is expressed here is Ransom's very theory of poetry. And while I am drawing parallels, I might point out that Ransom and Mann are ironists of the same strain, because they are dualists in common: compare Mann's treatment of death in *The Magic Mountain*.

28. *Stories of Three Decades*, trans. H. T. Lowe-Porter (New York: Alfred A. Knopf, 1951), pp. 102–103.

Ransom's poem is the story of what happens between a painter and his model on a spring day, and what happens to his painting. The warmth of spring is contrasted to the coldness of the artist's eye—the "Northern light"; until this day the painter has been able to "limn the dream aright / In his honest Northern light."

> He had nearly done his portrait,
> But there came a day in April;
> There was treachery come winging
> On the dust of flowers springing;
> It was not a day for artist to play host
> Lest the man come uppermost.
>
> And he knew that he was changed,
> Was changed the wintry lady.
> It was but their way of speaking,
> It was but their way of looking,
> But the cunning all had fled his fingertips;
> So he bent and kissed her lips.
>
> Then for all his giddy pulses
> He laid grim hands on the picture,
> And he trampled it with loathing,
> Flung it many miles to nothing,
> And it screamed to wake the devils as it fell
> Till it thundered into hell.
>
> Then a silence straightway took them
> And they paced the woodland homeward.
> What a bitter noon in April
> (It was April, it was April)
> As she touched his fleeting fingers cold as ice
> And recited, "It was nice!"

The difference between Ransom's view of the artist and Mann's is that Ransom's painter is not a kind of outlaw (it will be remembered that Tonio Kröger, symbolically, is almost arrested on returning to his home town). The painter is almost a religious, for he has, if not a vision, a "dream" and an "honest . . . light"; and when he betrays it the poem invokes hell and the devils. At the end of the poem the artist is uppermost again: the fingers that had lost their cunning are now icy. All the difference between him and the "normal" lady is in her trite, her "recited" word *nice*: an ironic difference that still, however, allows for a little pathos in her situation as well.

It is not a remarkable poem texturally, but it is an interesting poem, what Auden calls the "Prospero-dominated" poem: the poem whose reason for being is chiefly its theme—assuming, of course, that it is at least well written—as distinguished from the "Ariel-dominated" poem, the verbal delight, the pure poem.

In "Blackberry Winter," on the other hand, there are tastes of vintage Ransom, though the theme is well enough represented among the selected poems.

> If the lady hath any loveliness, let it die.
> For being drunken with the steam of Cuban cigars,
> I find no pungence in the odour of stars,
> And all my music goes out of me on a sigh.

If in comparison some of the poem is a little diffuse and abstract, it still is a successful poem. Its theme is the modern age. Romantic love has given way to barnyard naturalism:

> Fiercely the pale youth clambered to her, till—
> Hoarsely the rooster awakened him, footing the mould.

And "all of the wars have dwindled since Troy fell." But like the persistent explorer, though the golden and silver ages are past, and the goddesses dead who competed in beauty for the golden apple, the bemused modern has a little hope:

> But still would I sing to my maidenly apple-tree
> Before she has borne me a single apple of red;
> The pictures of silver and apples of gold are dead;
> But one more apple ripeneth yet maybe.
>   .   .   .   .   .   .
> But still I will haunt beneath my apple-tree,
> Heedful again to star-looks and wind-words,
> Anxious for the flash of whether eyes or swords,
> And hoping a little, a little, that either may be.

The title poem of *Two Gentlemen in Bonds* is a group of twenty sonnets set in medieval times and concerned with two brothers, co-inheritors of their father's estate: Paul, a man of large animal appetites, an athlete, an extrovert—"a smile always in waiting"—and at the end something of a politician; and Abbott, a thin and pale intellectual who

> could talk in Latin, music, mime,
> Or sonneteer with Petrarch in his prime.
> He had a prince's powers, but what he willed
> Was to go down to dust with the unfulfilled
> Rather than stint himself with space and time.

When the king pays them a visit, Abbott, rather than pay obsequious homage and be part of vulgar entertainments, moves to the tower and there decides to remain for good, dedicated to meditation and misanthropy. Paul, left to play host alone, wins the king's favor and with the royal blessing marries his beautiful cousin Edith, who before had been somewhat undecided between him and Abbott: "How noble is man thinking," she once had said. At the end of the sequence, the notoriety of the brothers,

> Paul waxing great and thirsting for the power,
> Abbott a death's-head gibing from a tower,

has awakened the spirit of their father, who may well be God the Father contemplating the split nature of his human progeny:

> "Now I remember life; and out of me
> Lawfully leaping, the twin seed of my loins,
> Brethren, whom no split fatherhood disjoins;
> But in the woman's house how hatefully
> They trod upon each other! till now I see
> My manhood halved and squandered, two heads, two hearts,
> Each partial son despising the other's parts;
> And so it is, and so it always will be."

That is the final sonnet, but the theme is just as clear in the first sonnet. Because it is and because there is little story and no characterization beyond the outlining of the two types, the result is repetition of the obvious. But there are fine passages. The sonnet "Rain," a speech by Abbott, can stand alone and was in fact printed separately under another title.[29] It concludes in imagery unusually striking for Ransom:

> "Think of the happy dead men lying in ponds
> Filled of rainwater—eyeballs rolling wide
> In the comfort of that undusty unlit tide—
> Ears flowered green and huge beyond the bawling
> That shook the air of earth—tumbled, or crawling
> On naked legs among the lily-fronds."

What is without doubt the best sonnet unfortunately cannot be separated. It is "Epithalamion of a Peach," an extended conceit built on Paul's eating of a peach.

> She was small, ripe, round, a maid not maculate
> Saving her bright cheeks, but the rude bridegroom
> Claims her, his heavy hand has led her home.
> Nor did he pull her gently through his gate
> As had a lover dainty and delicate:
> The two-and-thirty cut-throats doing his will
> Tore off her robe and stripped her bare until
> Drunken with appetite, he devoured and ate.

Two other poems in the volume also are concerned with Abbott's type of exile, an exile of which the intellectual in his excursions outside space and time is always in danger. "Miller's Daughter" is really about an admirer of the blue-eyed miller's daughter, a self-confessed

> poor bookish hind,
> Who come by fabulous roads around the hill
> To bring the famous daughter of the mill
> No combs to sell, no corn to grind,
>
> But too much pudding in my head
> Of learned characters and scraps of love.

In part he sees her, as we say, "for herself"—exciting with the mystery of her individuality, her own beauty:

> I have seen, O, the miller's daughter
> And on her neck a coral necklace lies
> And yellow glint of corn is in her eyes
> Which are a blue stillwater.

29. "Proud Heart Rained Upon," *The Measure*, No. 52 (June, 1925), p. 11.

Here the comparisons are from nature. But in part he sees her merely as an illustration of abstract properties in his head: "primary chrome of hair, / Astronomied Oes of eyes." And here the comparisons are from "the worldless heavens." (The phrase is from Tate's "The Subway," another poem about abstraction.) She illustrates for him the idea Woman; and though she is exciting in this way too, the excitement is adolescent:

> What then to do but stare—
> A learned eye of our most Christian nation
> And foremost philosophical generation—
> At primary chrome of hair,
>
> Astronomied Oes of eyes
> And the white moons I tremble to behold
> (More than my books did shake me, or a tale told)
> And all her parts likewise.

Mrs. Cowan tells us that the semi-centennial celebration of Vanderbilt University occasioned the poem about the intellect titled "Semi-Centennial." Since the poem was first printed in *The Fugitive*, the second line seems to contain another local allusion, playful in its half-relevance:

> When the green army battled and drove North
> The black army, one old fugitive crept forth
> From his hole beside the hearth, wearied a little
> With fixing his blue eye on ash and spittle.

This is the intellectual, who is observing, unimpressed, his fiftieth spring; unimpressed because his own head has given birth to greater glories:

> He was a small man with head larger than most,
> And so much it had kept, and so much lost,
> It could not buzz and spin with giddy mirth
> At these quick salad hues that gauded earth.
>
> Business brighter than that had been enacted
> Day after day within the curled compacted
> Grey hemispheres—music and histories
> Enveloping more than April novelties.

If the grey cloud of thought for once was stilled
At the great cycle fifty times fulfilled,
Yet it was feathers that quivered, grass, the bee,
The foal, the firstling yellow bloom—not he.

He leaned upon the earth and turned his eyes
About the world and said with no surprise—
"I am a god. I may not seem to be,
The other gods have disinherited me.

. . . . . .

"The better part of godhead is design.
This is not theirs only, for I know mine,
And I project such worlds as need not yield
To this commanded April on the field."

. . . . . .

And he watched, with large head resting in the sun,
The gods at play, and did not envy one.
He had the magic too, and knew his power,
But was too tired to work it at that hour.

"Amphibious Crocodile" is a long and more broadly satiric
companion piece to "Philomela." Robert Crocodile, too, goes to
Europe in search of culture and grace and is frustrated.

Next on the grand tour is Westminster, and Fleet Street.
His Embassy must present him to King George.
Who is the gentleman whose teeth are so large?
That is Mr. Crocodile the renowned aesthete.

To know England really one must try the country
And the week-end parties; he is persuaded to straddle
A yellow beast in a red coat on a flat saddle.
Much too gymnastical are the English gentry.

Surely a scotch and soda with the Balliol men.
But when old Crocodile rises to speak at the Union
He is too miserably conscious of his bunion
And toes too large for the aesthetic regimen.

It is too too possible he has wandered far
From the simple center of his rugged nature.
I wonder, says he, if I am the sort of creature
To live by travel, projects, affaires de coeur?

Soberly Crocodile sips of the Eucharist.
But as he meditates the obscene complexes
And infinite involutions of the sexes,
Crocodile sets up for a psychoanalyst.

. . . . . .

But who would ever have thought it took such a strength
To whittle the tree of being to a point
While the deep-sea urge cries Largo, and every joint
Tingles with gross desire of lying at length?

. . . . . .

The earth spins from its poles and is glared on
By the fierce incessant suns, but here is news
For a note in the fine-print of the Thursday Reviews:
Old Robert Crocodile is packed up and gone.

His dear friends cannot find him. The ladies write
As usual but their lavender notes are returned
By the U. S. Postmaster and secretively burned.
He has successfully got out of sight.

Crocodile hangs his pretty clothes on a limb
And lies with his fathers, and with his mothers too,
And his brothers and sisters as it seems right to do;
The family religion is good enough for him.

Full length he lies and goes as water goes,
He weeps for joy and welters in the flood,
Floating he lies extended many a rood,
And quite invisible but for the end of his nose.

The metaphor of "the family religion" suggests one of the key
metaphors of "Philomela": "Never was she baptized."

"Moments of Minnie" is another "Prospero-dominated" poem,
and I wonder whether I may be the only reader of *Two Gentlemen in Bonds* who likes it, there being no mention of it among
Ransom's critics. Minnie's moments are a moment of pain and
a moment of happiness, neither of which feelings can Minnie
express in words. Minnie is not very intelligent. Also she is not
quite respectable.

We must not honor girls of Minnie's kind
Whose charms are more endearing than her mind.
We are the Christian moralists we are.

As the tone indicates, the poem is in part a defense of Minnie. Her "gallant meaning" has no words, but is in "the outleaning / Of her soft lips." And what her inarticulateness calls in question for the speaker, as he remembers the intensity of her feelings, is not her intelligence, but the further boundaries of rational discourse (and, by implication, of moral categories). "Pain is primitive," and finally inexpressible.

> Oh, Oh, Oh! Not a word, not a name,
> And no tears flowed, yet wry and dry it came
> Till I trembled—and I fled.

So, too, is love; its sound is no "lettered word."

> Then I washed my mind with its old memories.
> For it was better to reconstitute the trees
> And the bridegroom scarlet bird of April crying
> To his brown one embowered, and the flying
> Mirth that bubbled off this woman's mouth
> From secret wells abundant as the South
> Which spilled their joy too thickly for sharp speech.
> Ah, Ah, Ah! she sighed deeply, and each
> Breathing was a new Ah! until I heard
> What never issues on a lettered word.

The inverse statement of this poem's theme might be extended a little into a statement about Ransom's kind of poetry. Since language has its limits (the unstated argument behind his poems runs), its best use is the exact expression of attitudes, rather than the attempted expression of the whole range of experience. So the subjects of the poems are the entities that have names, not the wells secret as dreams that may issue only as a flow of image, and the poems themselves a kind of ideal discourse directed to an ideally civilized circle of men and women—ourselves at *our* best moments. Just as the acknowledgement of deeper sources of being would be tacit among the ideal circle, since these people would also be wise, so is it tacit in the poems. But it is not expressed. That is one reason that the reader who wants before anything else exciting imagery, the imagery of a Roethke, will not find it in Ransom.

Chills and Fever and *Two Gentlemen in Bonds* are Ransom's central achievement as a writer. Although there are only ninety-nine poems in the two volumes and no broad range of theme, there is a remarkably rich variety of poetic experience among them (the difference between "Captain Carpenter" and "Vision by Sweetwater," to name two at random) as I hope I have demonstrated along the way, in trying to demonstrate in the critic's narrow room their high quality and their ultimate seriousness.

Chapter IV

The Later Poems

THE few poems in *Selected Poems* written in the thirty-six years following *Two Gentlemen in Bonds* are, as we would expect, highly skillful performances, except for the latest two. But they are not distinctive poems. In fact, one wonders whether his closest readers, coming across these poems in quarterlies and magazines, could have identified their author if they had not carried his name. These are the last seven in the 1963 *Selected Poems:* "Prelude to an Evening," "What Ducks Require," "Of Margaret," "Painted Head," "Address to the Scholars of New England," "Master's in the Garden Again," and "Prelude to an Evening: Revised and Explicated." In truth these are only five, since there are two "Preludes" and "Master's in the Garden Again" is a new version of "Conrad in Twilight," which first appeared in 1923.

On the revised version of "Prelude to an Evening" and on "Master's in the Garden Again" we have extensive comments by the poet himself.

The revision of "Prelude" must have one of the most remarkable histories to be found in poetry—a history that recalls the old serial novels, like *The Return of the Native,* whose readers demanded a new and happier ending. In the earlier "Prelude" a young husband returns at evening to his household possessed by a sense of the world's evil, and obsessed, almost, with his own taint:

> Do not enforce the tired wolf
> Dragging his infected wound homeward
> To sit tonight with the warm children
> Naming the pretty kings of France.

He considers sharing his vision with his wife, a little envious perhaps of her appearance of innocence as she tends the children, or perhaps exasperated with her innocence. He imagines what it would be like if his terrible thoughts should become her thoughts. It would not be like a nightmare—nothing so tame as that,

> For cry, cock-crow, or the iron bell
> Can crack the sleep-sense of outrage.

It would be a pervasive sense of evil, a part even of her most innocent domestic movements:

> There is a drift of fog on your mornings;
> You in your peignoir, dainty at your orange-cup,
> Feel poising round the sunny room
>
> Invisible evil, deprived, and bold.
>   · · · · · ·
> Freshening the water in the blue bowls
> For the buckberries with not all your love,
> You shall be listening for the low wind,
> The warning sibilance of pines.
>
> You like a waning moon, and I accusing
> Our too banded Eumenides,
> You shall make Noes but wanderingly,
> Smoothing the heads of the hungry children.

That is the way the poem ends. Only a year before he published his radical revision, Ransom was saying that it was his favorite among his own poems:

Because it is "pure" as many of this poet's poems are not, in the sense that there is no particular moral or philosophy attaching to it; and because it is open at the end, in the sense that the reader may imagine if he wishes that the speaker by expressing himself has gained some relief, and now is capable of baby-sitting, or whether he has now involved his mate likewise in his own poor spirits.[1]

But he tells us in his essay on the new version that it had become "disagreeable to my ears as I continued to read it on public occasions now and then," because of the speaker's character:

He seems to think he will win her over; there is no intimation that it may turn out quite differently. But suppose he succeeds: will not that be a dreary fate for the woman? And what of the children? Those are not his questions. But they came to be mine. By the end of the ninth stanza he pictures her prophetically as rapt in her new terrors, almost to the point of forgetting the children; if they are hungry, she will absent-mindedly smooth their heads. . . .
    I had not come to saying that the man was odious, that he was, incontestably, the villain. That was rather strange.[2]

Now the remarkable part of this history:

One day last winter, what I had not said was said for me; by a strong-minded young woman writing in a very little magazine devoted to the "explication" of difficult verse, in answer to a subscriber's query. What did the man of my poem mean to do? She replied with a commendable severity: this man was simply a brutal character who meant not to do any baby-sitting even if the babies were his own. At once I conceded the justice of her observation, and with more relief than surprise.[3]

Here is the judgment of the strong-minded young woman writing in *The Explicator:*

Cleanth Brooks . . . speaks of the "tenderness" with which the husband regards his wife's confusion and agitation as she goes about the house all day. I am unable to detect that emotion in the husband. His comments seem to be a clinical psychoanalysis of his wife's "brief enchanted headful." . . . He has a feeling of guilt ("I accusing / Our too banded Eumenides") and even admires her fortitude in the face of her uneasiness ("your gallant fear"); yet his perverse nature does

1. Note to "Prelude to an Evening," *Poet's Choice,* ed. Paul Engle and Joseph Langland (New York: The Dial Press, 1962), p. 13.
2. *Selected Poems: A Revised and Enlarged Edition* (New York: Alfred A. Knopf, 1964), pp. 102–103.
3. *Ibid.,* p. 103.

not allow him to do anything to dispel "the drift of fog" on her mornings. . . . He is a wolf, aloof and undomesticated; he would lick his wound in the wilderness rather than drag it home to the fireside as a dog would. In fact, his distance from the entire domestic condition is suggested in his request that he not be enforced to sit tonight with the warm, sticky children climbing over him coaxing him to read them stories from their picture-books "Naming the pretty kings of France" with their long curly hair and ruffled collars.[4]

And Ransom continues:

All the same, I was soon wondering if I might not somehow patch up the poem and save it; by saving the woman and the children from their distress; and of course by saving the villain too, who so far as the genders go belonged to my party. I rather thought not. If I must administer to him a speedy and radical "conversion" after many stanzas of villainy—the idea was too forbidding.[5]

The solution he believes that he has found has also an odd source, significantly abstract: a chapter from an unfinished study by the late Charles Coffin, a colleague at Kenyon, of the theology of *Paradise Lost*. What he has found in Coffin's study, however, is not really a solution: the conversion still is speedy, and difficult to believe. He has found only a theological argument for the desired conversion. And it might be added that while the theology is highly interesting, the following explication that Ransom bases on it is not an explication of the actual poem, but of the intended poem.

The characters are symbolic: they are Adam and Eve, the essential man and the essential woman. Adam according to Coffin was created free; but Ransom prefers to say that he was created only half free since he was appointed with a body that operates rather independently of the rest of him and at the same time is severely limited, unable to respond, fortunately, to every impulse of Adam's unlimited imagination. The relevance of this part of his analysis lies, I think, in stanza ten, to which he ascribes an erotic motive:

4. Virginia L. Peck, "Ransom's 'Prelude to an Evening,'" *The Explicator*, XX, No. 5 (Jan., 1962), Item 41.
5. *Selected Poems: A Revised and Enlarged Edition*, p. 103.

I would have us magnificent at my coming;
Two souls tight-clasped; and a swamp of horrors.
O you shall be handsome and brave at fearing.
Now my step quickens . . .

More important for his explication is the character of Eve. She, Ransom agrees with Coffin, was created with only half the freedom Adam enjoys, for she was not given his powers of intellect and imagination; when her husband and Raphael begin to talk metaphysics, she quietly leaves. God did not make her an entirely compatible mate for Adam (His little joke on Adam, who asked for her to begin with, Ransom suggests). So in the first eight stanzas of the poem:

The matter turns on whether she is free to respond to the interests of her spouse as an artist; whose art this time is an extravagant "supposal" or fantasy, having a theological cast and an evil imagination. Is she capable of being swept off her feet by a work of art—especially one that invokes a vision of evil? Adam hopes to find her capable. But the answer is in the new stanzas. He concedes that she is not capable; he will not ask of her the impossible.[6]

The other source of difficulty between them is the maternal interests which occupy Eve in place of metaphysics. Frustratingly for Adam, once Eve has tempted him and the children have come, they become her major interest and almost her only interest, so that it must now be Adam who "solicits" Eve:

Let her share his professional interests; then she will have his preoccupations, sometimes as evil as they will be good, but she will also have him; he may even suggest that less time should be spent with the children. But, even before Adam comes into her presence to make his proposition, he is condemned out of his own mouth. The children must occupy her mind now; they have replaced their father in her deepest affections; and if he desires her favors he will have to take them not on his terms but on hers, which will stipulate that he must share the responsibility for the children.[7]

So as his "step quickens," suddenly Adam "comes to his senses and knows that Eve will never accept his invitation; not the

6. *Ibid.*, p. 108.
7. *Ibid.*, p. 110.

open and intellectual part, not the implicit erotic part if that is bound up with the other."[8]

This is more than interesting: it is true, I am certain, as a description of man and woman and the best relations possible between them. But the description did not find its way into the poem. "In a true poem," Ransom writes before beginning his explication,

it is as if the religious dogma or the moral maxim had been dropped into the pot as soon as the act of composition began; sinking down out of sight and consciousness, it is as if it became a fluid and was transfused into the bloodstream of the poet now, and would be communicated to the bloodstream of his auditors eventually. The significance of the poem is received by feeling; or, more technically, by immediate unconscious intuition.[9]

And further on he says:

It is more faithful to the sense of a serious poem to translate it into theology, if we must translate it, than into morality.[10]

Here is the way the new version ends, beginning with Adam's quickening step:

Now my step quickens; and meets a huge No!

Whose No was it? like the hoarse policeman's,
Clopping onstage in the Name of the Law.
That was Me; forbidding tricks at homecoming;
At the moment of coming to its white threshold.

I went to the nations of disorder
To be freed of the memory of good and evil;
There even your image was disfigured;
Then the boulevards rocked; they said, Go back.

I am here; and to balk my ruffian I bite
The tongue devising all that treason;
Then creep in my wounds to the sovereign flare
Of the room where you shine on the good children.

8. *Ibid.*, p. 111.
9. *Ibid.*, p. 105.
10. *Ibid.*, p. 106.

I am certain that Ransom's account of the true poem does not describe his composition of his new ending, as I am certain it does not describe the experience of its reader. In this case the poet was conscious of the theology to begin with. Yet he scarcely began to make it dramatic or immediate in the poem, so that in explicating the poem Ransom is not, as he would like to believe, translating into prose terms, theological terms, a significance that the reader has gotten by "immediate unconscious intuition": all of the theology is in the essay, which, like one of Shaw's prefaces, is more interesting than the imaginative work. The work itself translates into morality instead of into theology: that is, into a dictum, rather than into a statement about the nature of things. Whereas Adam in the essay or in the intended poem says in effect, "Eve is no intellectual, but she is a good mother, and after all I can't change her nature"; in the actual poem he says, "I must behave myself, for Eve is Sacred Motherhood." For the motive of his conversion in the poem is not his understanding of Eve's nature, but only his vaudeville policeman of a conscience. (I would like to imagine that the policeman's slapstick entrance reflects the poet's embarrassment at what he has done to his poem.) True, Eve—with "the good children"—is behind the conscience, but only as the angelic light of the final line. Our objection to the closing lines Ransom has anticipated, in calling them "perhaps half maudlin."[11] But the objection remains, and the author of "Vaunting Oak," "Parting, without a Sequel," "Two in August," and like poems will understand if we are more convinced of the reality of the atmosphere in the old version, than of the domesticity, as pure and shining as the faces on a Norman Rockwell painting, at the conclusion of the new.

I think there is more to be said on behalf of the old poem, however, than something to the effect that it is more believable, and interesting, because given to the devil's portrait. For this poem of which the poet in his elder years has thought he must feel ashamed, I offer in fact a "theological" defense. The poem is not simply about a husband's villainous and undomesticated

11. *Ibid.*, p. 111.

imagination. At least as vivid in the husband's imagination as the evil is his wife's courage and dignity in its presence, a courage she keeps despite the frailty which he pictures to himself—and this is where I see tenderness—in her wandering Noes and her abstracted stroking of the children's heads. The courage and dignity are implicit in the lines quoted at the beginning of this discussion, and explicit in these:

> All day the clock will metronome
> Your gallant fear; the needles clicking,
> The heels detonating the stair's cavern.

An idea of the wife's dignity, as a matter of fact, is the chief reason Ransom gives for what he now describes as his immoderate fondness for the old poem:

I suppose a poet is excused without having to invoke the Fifth Amendment if he believes in his own poem, at least at the stage of first publication. My liking went quite beyond its merits, and lasted much too long. It had to do with some notion of a workmanlike poetic line carrying forward the argument while the woman was being borne through successive terrors not of her own making, yet still invested in her incorruptible dignity. It was with intense pleasure that I watched her suffering there; she was a heroine almost after the pattern of some diminutive classical tragedy.[12]

He writes as though the dignity had been entirely in his mind, but it clearly is in the poem and one of its major effects. What is its point? I hope that it is not also perverse to suppose that the husband would quite properly see his wife as a more complete woman, a more adult companion, for having his own dark knowledge; that therefore the poem is one in theme with those in *Chills and Fever* and *Two Gentlemen in Bonds* in which innocence is instructed in mortality and evil, for its own good. (Eve would not have to be an intellectual to learn this much.) Ransom has suggested a comparison with one of those poems himself, though to another purpose:

I believe I have only one other poem so vindictive as this, and I know some readers to whom it is no secret which it must be. It is

12. *Ibid.,* pp. 102–103.

the one called "Blue Girls," where the girls in the schoolyard are preening themselves in their beauty (as they should) till a man looking on addresses them and forces them to take account of a blear-eyed old woman whom he invents on the spot, and describes, with the threat that to her favor they must come soon.[13]

His purpose is not quite serious, obviously: is it another embarrassed joke, like the one about Adam's conscience? For he has not set a guilty hand to the revision of "Blue Girls."

In style the new stanzas of "Prelude" share an odd quality with his other new piece of verse, "Master's in the Garden Again": a choppiness and prosiness that are almost anti-style, as though the poet were not only impatient of all but his abstract meaning, but even a little distrustful of the graces that once composed his style. He describes the new stanzas as "like the others in form, being quatrains of unrhymed four-beat lines which mostly are end-stopped."[14] But the preponderance of end-stopped lines is in the new stanzas. In addition there are numerous stops within the lines, the result of very brief phrases and clauses:

> Whose No was it? || like the hoarse policeman's, ||
> Clopping onstage in the Name of the Law. ||
> That was Me; || forbidding tricks at homecoming; ||
> At the moment of coming to its white threshold.

The changes he has made in the original eight stanzas are to the same effect and in addition prefer the prose idea to the concrete detail. The most unhappy change, I think, was in these lines:

> But now, by our perverse supposal,
> There is a drift of fog on your mornings;
> You in your peignoir, dainty at your orange-cup,
> Feel poising round the sunny room
>
> Invisible evil, deprived, and bold.

13. *Ibid.*, p. 103.
14. *Ibid.*, p. 101.

They now read:

> And now? To confirm our strange supposal,
> Apparitions wait upon sunny mornings;
> You in your peignoir commend the heaped oranges
> Gold on the platter for cheeky children
>
> But freeze at the turbulence under the floor.

"A drift of fog" colored the atmosphere of the wife's mornings;
"apparitions" merely names the evil. And in the next line, "You
in your peignoir, dainty at your orange-cup," the effect was an
elegance and a femininity poignant in their vulnerability to the
envisioned evil.[15] Now "dainty" and "orange-cup" are replaced
by "commend" and "heaped oranges"; the idea is uppermost,
and we know what idea the poet has in mind: Eve as *mater
familias,* bountiful and devoted. The new words protest too
much, I think, especially *commend.* Its Biblical quality ("into
Thy hands I commend my spirit") suggests a little ceremony,
a kind of blessing of the oranges—certainly more than Eve's
merely passing them, or *re*commending them.

Another change has not even the idea in mind: the change of
the line "You shall make Noes but wanderingly," to "You
making Noes but they lack conviction." "Wanderingly" suggests
a little scene: the woman wandering a few steps here or there
in the room, uncertain, distracted. And the line has a little
music, its stressed syllables—two of them in "wanderingly"—a
distinct ripple upon the surface of the unstressed. The only
principle discernible in the revision is a preference for the
flat prose statement. This is a style, or non-style, different not
only from that of *Chills and Fever* and *Two Gentlemen in
Bonds,* but from the "newer" style of the first "Prelude," "What

15. These lines probably owe something to Wallace Stevens's "Sunday
Morning":

> Complacencies of the peignoir, and late
> Coffee and oranges in a sunny chair . . .

Ransom admires the poem as "one of the most elegant poems in the language.
Easily the most elegant poem—unless it'd be another by Stevens—to appear
in America" (lecture at Vanderbilt University, 1961).

Ducks Require," and the others of the 1927–1939 period. It seems the style of a prose writer doing a little reluctant versifying.

Except for its rhymes and the five lines kept intact from the old "Conrad in Twilight," "Master's in the Garden Again" is in the same style, on which Ransom himself had a half-rueful comment to make after three other members of a symposium had discussed the poem:

> What can a poet do without critics to advise him what he is doing? and without critics to pass over in silence some of his favorite passages and by that silence tell him that he has not done what he thought he was doing? I can imagine that this latter testimony is one that happens often to poets who try to do only wonderful things, and discover from the general silence that poetry for them is tense, terse, and jerky, and that they do not address themselves to the general intelligence.[16]

However, he also says that he has not yet made up his mind about the success of his latest poem.[17]

The Master of the poem, who is still Conrad,[18] sits in his garden on a cold and damp fall day and pleasantly resists his wife's pleasant nagging to come inside:

> "You're lonely, my loony? Your house is up there.
> Go and wait. If you won't, I'll go jump in the lake."

The wife offstage, the poet now describes the autumn, getting most of the lines from the fine final section of "Conrad in Twilight." These are the best lines of the new poem as well, but they have a strange flavor sandwiched between two courses of the plainer fare Ransom now prefers to serve us. Lines three through seven are unaltered:

> And the master's back has not uncurved
> Nor the autumn's blow for an instant swerved.

16. "And Now the Grateful Author," *The Contemporary Poet* . . . , p. 134.
17. *Ibid.*, p. 135.
18. "To the best of my knowledge I had chosen that name, in the early 1920's, because it had been the pen-name of a brooding and intellectual Pole who wrote novels, and I happened to have been born in a town called Pulaski, about sixty miles from where I wrote" (*ibid.*, p. 136).

> Autumn days in our section
> Are the most used-up thing on earth
> (Or in the waters under the earth)
> Having no more color nor predilection
> Than cornstalks too wet for the fire
> And black leaves pitched onto the byre.

> The show is of death. There is no defection.

In this mood Conrad is inspired to perform a little pantomime of defiance in the third and final section against whatever Power has killed the leaves ("By the bite of Its frost the children were lost"):

> See the tell-tale art of the champion heart.

> Here's temple and brow, which frown like the law.
> If the arm lies low, yet the rage looks high.
> The accusing eye? that's a fierce round O.
> The offense was raw, says the fix in the jaw.
> We'll raise a rare row! we'll heave a brave blow!

> A pantomime blow, if it damns him to do,
> A yell mumming too. But it's gay garden now,
> Play sweeter than pray, that the darkened be gay.

"The garden is gay, if it can be gay," Ransom explicates,

because the hero has performed his action, though it was only a symbolic action, in a sort of grand style, making something out of a barren occasion. And in the last line, with "Play sweeter than pray," the author has imagined himself as on the track of an incipient law for poetry, a way of distinguishing itself from theology when theology has failed the poet: to play the thing that we cannot pray.[19]

19. *Ibid.*, p. 140. "The title which I gave to the poem, . . . and the dedication to Thomas Hardy, jumped into my consciousness simultaneously out of the memory of a slight but touching poem of his entitled 'The Master and the Leaves.' . . . My imagination, while I was working on the present poem, would sometimes picture for me the aging but not yet aged Mr. T. H. sitting drooped on a wet stone in a prospect of fallen leaves, and maintaining his posture with only the slightest variation while he talked with his wife Emma, then brooded awhile, and finally in his solitary rage made his play against the Immanent Will" (pp. 135–136).

"Conrad in Twilight" seems an incomplete poem ("rather ignominious"[20] Ransom calls it, though he has kept it in the *Selected Poems*). The final section, as fine a passage as it is in
itself, does not develop out of the playfully mocking jingle of
the preceding lines—

> Conrad's house has thick red walls,
> The log on Conrad's hearth is blazing,
> Slippers and pipe and tea are served,
> Butter and toast are meant for pleasing!

It does not conclude the poem, it simply ends it. But how successful is the new version? Ransom, more critic than poet in
these two recent compositions, is ahead of us in putting his finger
on the crucial point: "the man's peculiar pantomime at the
end. . . . Is it worth the bluster and the bother it has cost him,
even if at last it can take place in the secrecy of his garden?
Is it either probable or possible?"[21] His hope is that the virtuos-
ity of the verse itself—though modestly he does not use that
word—will sweep the reader along and make the Master's little
ritual seem credible and in some way important.

We know how much is done by sheer stylization when the storyteller
would have us believe in his unsubstantial ghost, or some phantasy
with many characters. . . . In the five lines of the pantomime where
we see Conrad's features working in silhouette, and even in the final
three lines which follow in the author's official voice, we have a very
special prosodical variation. . . . All the sixteen rhyme-places, half
in the middle and half at the ends, are supplied with long open vowels,
which have no consonants after them or else silent consonants. Sixteen
rhyming syllables, yes, sixteen monosyllables, fill those places, and
show six different rhymes based on the following words, which are
not given in the order in which they appear: *law, low, high, now,
do, gay.* It used to be the understanding among poets that any two
long open syllables at the right places would be construed as rhyming,
but that is unnecessary here, where each one can find a rhyming
partner, sometimes more than one. I shall not tell of the pain this
pattern required of its composer, nor the joy when it began to work
out.[22]

20. *Selected Poems: A Revised and Enlarged Edition,* p. vi.
21. *The Contemporary Poet . . . ,* p. 134.
22. *Ibid.,* pp. 139–140.

But, alas, a rhyme scheme is only a rhyme scheme and by itself
works no magic, without the charm of phrase and the seductive
sophistication of tone that capture the reader in the old poems.
So barely represented, Conrad's mute gesturing seems only a
little silly.

It is significant that Ransom should describe the poem as
his "first." ("I mean the first made by my present Self, who
has grown out of the several other Selves during the years of
no poetry; made with all that awkwardness when one tries for
the first time to fashion some difficult kind of thing.")[23] For
his fault in this as in the new stanzas of "Prelude to an Evening"
is one more usual with the beginning writer: committing only
part of his idea to paper, and in the excitement of composition
thinking that he has committed it all. Another example is in
the dialogue between Conrad and his wife.

> "Conrad! dear man, surprise! aren't you bold
> To be sitting so late in your sodden garden?"

> "Woman! intrusion! does this promise well?
> I'm nursing my knees, they are not very cold.
> Have you known the fall of the year when it fell?
> Indeed it's a garden, but if you will pardon,
> The health of a garden is reason's burden."

That is enough for illustration. The wife's few lines are unrhymed, Ransom points out, while Conrad's are rhymed, and
Ransom intended that the reader should notice this difference
and see some significance in it (though to the reader accustomed
to Ransom's rhyming, three end-words in the wife's second
speech look like slant rhymes: *muck, neck, sake*).

Conrad is a poet and his wife is not; he rhymes easily, but she
has no knack for it. So the naughty man means to hear out her
unrhymed lines, then cap them with a group of lines that supply
rhyme-mates for hers, and for good measure some rhymed lines entirely his own. . . . But in my obstinate economy of words I blun-
dered here. I should have supplied an ampler leisure, and more and
successively clearer examples of the rhyme game.[24]

23. *Ibid.*, p. 134.
24. *Ibid.*, p. 137.

A rare poet, like Ransom's fellow Fugitive Donald Davidson, does his finest work after sixty; the reasons would be rewarding to explore. Far more usual is the poet for whom his admirers must feel a little embarrassed at the performances of his old age. (Wordsworth comes first to mind.) They will think it better had he not written again at all, and will not be expected to take much relish in showing why.

For the remainder of these poems, those composed between 1927 and 1939, we need feel no embarrassment at all—they are finished in sense and in style—though as I have said they offer little of the true Ransom flavor.

"What Ducks Require" belongs to the small group of his "romantic" poems. Its theme is in D. H. Lawrence: Thank God the universe is nonhuman.

One day as they were walking along the lane, they saw a robin sitting on the top twig of a bush, singing shrilly. The sisters stood to look at him. An ironical smile flickered on Gudrun's face.

"Doesn't he feel important?" smiled Gudrun.

"Doesn't he!" exclaimed Ursula, with a little ironical grimace. "Isn't he a little Lloyd George of the air!"

"Isn't he! Little Lloyd George of the air! That's just what they are," cried Gudrun in delight. Then for days, Ursula saw the persistent, obtrusive birds as stout, short politicians lifting up their voices from the platform, little men who must make themselves heard at any cost.

But . . . there came the revulsion. Some yellow-hammers suddenly shot along the road in front of her. And they looked to her so uncanny and inhuman, like flaring yellow barbs shooting through the air on some weird, living errand, that she said to herself: "After all, it is impudence to call them little Lloyd Georges. They are really unknown to us, they are the unknown forces. It is impudence to look at them as if they were the same as human beings. They are of another world. How stupid anthropomorphism is! Gudrun is really impudent, insolent, making herself the measure of everything, making everything come down to human standards. . . . The universe is nonhuman, thank God."[25]

25. D. H. Lawrence, *Women in Love* (New York: Modern Library, n. d.), p. 301.

The poem is a celebration of the duck and of the unknown forces of which like Lawrence's yellow-hammer he is a part. Some of his mysteriousness resides in his definable differences from man, who is represented by "lewd eye and fowler's gun," "ship and sail," "wharves," and "mortises and slate," and whose god is Lar. "Ducks require no ship and sail," and they are only "half-householders"—suggesting the sentiment of "Old Man Playing with Children"—they

> Beam their floor with ribs of grass,
> Disdain your mortises and slate
> And Lar who invalided lies.

Their nest is in the marsh which "quakes dangerous, the port / Where wet and dry precisely start." The marsh represents the very heart of the earth—its quaking perhaps like the heart's beating—a mixture of wet and dry, sea and land, both homes to the duck. But the essence of the duck, and therefore of his world, is undefinable: he ranges "in his wide degrees" beyond the conceptual. The duck newly hatched is "the infant prod-igy"—*prodigy* in the sense of the marvelous, going back to the Latin *prodigium*, "prophetic sign." Launched from his nest, he is

> Prodigious in his wide degrees
> Who where the winds and waters blow
> On raveling banks of fissured seas
> In reeds nestles, or will rise and go
> Where Capricornus dips his hooves
> In the blue chasm of no wharves.

The best of these poems, I think, is "Of Margaret," for which Ransom adopted the young girl who mourns the falling leaves in Hopkins's "Spring and Fall: to a Young Child." The theme of Hopkins's poem would obviously appeal to Ransom:

> It is the blight man was born for,
> It is Margaret you mourn for.

It might be the conclusion of one of his own pedagogical pieces. But his purpose in this instance is different: he does not mean merely to rewrite Hopkins's poem. Rather than instruct her inno-

cence, he means to pay its purity a tribute, and at the end of
the poem to invoke, as it were, its blessing. He addresses her
at the end as a kind of priestess (she may be a little older in
this poem than in Hopkins's), for she represents to him the sacramental view of nature, and of life.

The first stanza quietly prepares for such a significance with
the single metaphor from the Eucharist: the "wafer body" for
the first fallen leaf.

> With the fall of the first leaf that winds rend
> She and the boughs trembled, and she would mourn
> The wafer body as an own first born.

The three middle stanzas elaborate the child metaphor (the
winds "unchild / Her of the sons of all her mothering") in order
to elaborate her purity. "Virgin" is the formal, the ritual name
by which she is addressed in the final stanza, and the quality
of her purity is this:

> No mother sorrow is but follows birth
> And beyond that, conception.
>
> . . . . . .
>
> But no evil shall spot this, Margaret's page,
> For her generations were of the head,
> The eyes, the tender fingers, not the blood,
> And the issue was all flowers and foliage.

Actual motherhood must bear responsibility for evil: for the
commitment of the new being to the mortality of the body and
the evil of the world; and for whatever evil, large or small,
he as one more imperfect human being must commit. But Margaret's motherhood, as it is of the mind and the feelings and
not the body, is free of that responsibility: a kind of virgin
birth, if we wish to extend the metaphor of the wafer, which
is her "own first born."

The final stanza:

> Virgin, whose image bent to the small grass
> I keep against this tide of wayfaring,
> O hear the maiden pageant ever sing
> Of that far away time of gentleness.

"Virgin," partly because of what has gone before, has the strongest religious connotations, and now the phrase "the maiden pageant" makes them ancient as well as Christian, extending "that far away time of gentleness" as far into the past as the Vestal Virgins. The poet's appeal to her, "O hear the maiden pageant ever sing," is on his own behalf too, that her image may continue to sustain him in the flux of time and in the flux that is the modern world (the context gives his wayfaring more than a literal significance). She is an intercessor for him, a kind of priestess, because of the purity of her mourning—it is *not* Margaret she mourns for in this poem—because of her continued reverence, "bent to the small grass," for the Creation of an unnamed God who could will such destruction. *Reverence,* however, is not the summary word used in the poem, but *gentleness,* a specific expression of the attitude of reverence; more important, the poem invites us to think of the older meaning of *gentle* as well: "noble." In both of these senses, but more broadly in the second, gentleness is an extension into conduct, into the affairs of men, of the sacramental view of nature. It is, sadly, an ideal that has had its most nearly complete realization in the past, in a "far away time," though to its music of the spirit, the maiden song, Margaret now moves, an image of a modern poet's private belief.

The meter and the rhyme scheme invite us to dwell to this extent on *gentleness,* I think, giving it an emphasis beyond what it would receive anyway as the final word of the poem. The emphasis consists in particular of a slightly unnatural stress on the word's last syllable, due to the meter which gives the word two of the line's five accents:

Ŏf thăt fár ă wáy tíme ŏf gén tlĕ néss;

and due to the rhyme scheme, which makes us articulate the syllable's imperfect pairing with *grass.*

Certainly in this stanza we receive the meaning by "immediate unconscious intuition," influenced as we must be by the elevation of the style. The style is untypical of Ransom, not in the way of the other late poems, but in the way of the epitaph to "The

Equilibrists." In these two passages he attains a higher level than his ironic style, excellent as that is: a level that might even be called close to the "sublime."[26]

The other two poems, "Painted Head" and "Address to the Scholars of New England," are exercises in his later style upon his old theme of body's war with soul or with mind. The terse unrhymed quatrains of "Painted Head" move abruptly and wittily through the ideas suggested by a hanging portrait. The painted head

> Smiles from the air a capital on no
> Column or a Platonic perhaps head
> On a canvas sky depending from nothing;
>
> Stirs up an old illusion of grandeur
> By tickling the instinct of heads to be
> Absolute and to try decapitation
> And to play truant from the body bush.

Plato is summoned, of course, because of his championship of reason and his devotion to the pure idea. Then it appears on closer study that this head is too happy to have been a Platonic head,

> Is nameless and has authored for the evil
> Historian headhunters neither book
> Nor state,

"neither book / Nor state" suggesting Plato's utopia of right reason *The Republic*. The painter's abstraction of the head from its body was only "capital irony by a loving hand / That knew the no treason of a head like this." The painter would on the other hand make an actual Platonic head pay penance for its defection by painting it "an unlovely head"—or so I read the following elliptical stanza:

> Makes repentance in an unlovely head
> For having vinegarly traduced the flesh
> Till, the hurt flesh recusing, the hard egg
> Is shrunken to its own deathlike surface.

26. This level in "Of Margaret" is the product of revision: see the appendix. Especially important is the deletion of the legalistic diction from line 18—"you are acquit of statute wrong"—apparently written out of the habit of his ironic style: it qualified the tone to no precise purpose.

Egg suggests "egghead," another bit of irreverence to go with the puns on capital. This style continues as under a tight restraint of logic, albeit witty, until the final stanza, where the verse takes a flight:

> Beauty is of body.
> The flesh contouring shallowly on a head
> Is a rock-garden needing body's love
> And best bodiness to colorify
>
> The big blue birds sitting and sea-shell flats
> And caves, and on the iron acropolis
> To spread the hyacinthine hair and rear
> The olive garden for the nightingales.

The blue birds would have to be the eyes, and I take the sea-shell flats to be the teeth and the caves the mouth and perhaps the ears. "The olive garden for the nightingales" is troublesome; the brain has been suggested. The principle point is that the olive garden, the nightingales, the acropolis (the Greek word literally means the "upper city"), and the hyacinthine hair all invoke the classical world for its ideal of harmony between body and mind. If the olive garden is the brain, the meaning is that the mind in fact needs "best bodiness" to function best, must be in harmony with the body to entertain the nightingale's song, which has approximately the same significance as in "Philomela." The result of disharmony may be "the holy megrims" (holy headaches, in an older sense of the word, as well as low spirits) suffered by the Puritan fathers who are the subject of "Address to the Scholars of New England."

The "Address" is the Harvard Phi Beta Kappa poem of 1939, and it seems a little odd for its occasion: it indicts the founders of the host university for giving ear to the "scandal-mongering" of Plato.

> There used to be debate of soul and body,
> The soul storming incontinent with shrew's tongue
> Against what natural brilliance body had loved.
>   .   .   .   .   .   .

> Plato, before Plotinus gentled him,
> Spoke the soul's part, and though its vice is known
> We're in his shadow still, and it appears
> Your founders most of all the nations held
> By his scandal-mongering, and established him.

The poem has the character of a little treatise on the Puritans' Platonism. The tone is dry, but not mockingly as of old; it has a somewhat scholarly dryness. It is hard to imagine the reader who could become as fond of this poem as of some of the older ones. But we must admire the mind and talent that have given the most abstract thoughts concrete and formal expression, and in that expression there is some pleasure if not the former magic. In the concrete details there is a sober exercise of wit:

> Thrifty and too proud were the sea-borne fathers
> Who fetched the Pure Idea in a bound box
> And fastened him in a steeple.
>
> .   .   .   .   .   .
>
> If once the entail shall come on raffish sons,
> Knife-wit scholar and merchant sharp in thumb,
> With positive steel they'll pry into the steeple,
> And blinking through the cracked ribs at the void
> A judgment laughter rakes the cynic sons.

The impressive tightness of form consists in the measuring of fourteen grammatical sentences each into one stanza of five pentameter lines, unrhymed but with the final word of the first line repeated as the final word of the fifth, as with *sons* in the stanza above.

Most of the first eleven stanzas are autonomous, each presenting a single complete statement of the theme; there is no development of the idea in the course of the poem. The first two stanzas submit an example of the New England character in Sarah Pierrepont, pious and on occasion enthusiastic wife of Jonathan Edwards:

> When Sarah Pierrepont let her spirit rage
> Her love and scorn refused the bauble earth
> (Which took bloom even here, under the Bear).

The distinction between North and South implied by the reference to the northern constellations is expanded in stanza six, which explains that the Puritan doctrine was more moderately interpreted in the temperate South:

> But like prevailing wind New England's honor
> Carried, and teased small Southern boys in school,
> Whose heads the temperate birds fleeing your winter
> Construed for, but the stiff heroes abashed
> With their frozen fingers and unearthly honor.

In the eleventh stanza (one may quote at random from the first eleven), the events "of war or bread, / The secular perforces and short speech" are described as

> labors surlily done with the left hand,
> The chief strength giddying with transcendent clouds.

Giddying is another instance of that double rightness we discover sometimes in Ransom's use of a word. Its present meaning tells us that the Puritans were out of their natural element in the "transcendent clouds"; its etymology goes back to the Old English *gydig*, related to *god*, meaning "god-possessed," "in a state of divine frenzy."

The final three stanzas bring us to the present and show its paradoxical resemblances to the past.

> The tangent Heavens mocked the fathers' strength,
> And how the young sons know it, and study now
> To take fresh conquest of the conquered earth,
> But they're too strong for that, you've seen them whip
> The laggard will to deeds of lunatic strength.
>
> To incline the powerful living unto peace
> With Heaven is easier now, with Earth is hard.

The sons' technological "deeds of lunatic strength" express only another abstract view of the physical world: the sons conquer with their science the earth their fathers "conquered" with their Platonism. Like their fathers' kind of abstractionism, theirs allows no peace, no harmony. Peace is "enforced" only by death, an attribute ironically of the scorned earth,

> A gentle Majesty, whose myrtle and rain
> Enforce the fathers' gravestones unto peace.

Just as the young ministers who graduated from Harvard College might have burned with the zeal of their gospel, so do their young descendents whose graduation ceremony the poet has just witnessed burn with the zeal of their twentieth-century enlightenment:

> I saw the youngling bachelors of Harvard
> Lit like torches, and scrambling to disperse
> Like aimless firebrands pitiful to slake, . . .

But their zeal is destructive: "aimless firebrands" parallels the phrase "lunatic strength" above. It is destructive in its purely practical view of nature, in its purely practical view of the whole of life: the opposite to the ideal celebrated in "Of Margaret." However,

> if there's passion enough for half their flame,
> Your wisdom has done this, sages of Harvard.

What has their wisdom done exactly? And what wisdom? The poem ends with somewhat the vagueness of a compliment murmured out of politeness. The meaning I think is this: If the dangerous zeal of the descendents, which to a degree is an inheritance of the rationalism in Puritan theology, is at least partly balanced by passion, which was an enemy of Plato as it is an enemy of an exploitive attitude toward nature and a pragmatic view of man, then the sages of Harvard may feel the pride at least of having contributed one half of a whole view of life.

If this impressive poem, and "Of Margaret," "What Ducks Require," "Painted Head," and the first "Prelude to an Evening" do not engage us except for certain passages as we feel we have a right to be engaged by a Ransom poem, they are an additional measure of a brilliant talent, and additional testimony to a whole view of life. Ransom's poems, it seems perfectly safe to predict, will be permanent in our literature: part of its "real" property, even though for the time of wayfaring present and ahead they may be only personal property of a few.

Revisions of
Twenty-one Poems

Shown below are the significant changes that Ransom has made from printing to printing in some of his most important poems. (Lines changed only in punctuation or capitalization are excluded.) Line numbers of each poem are those of the latest version, that of the 1963 *Selected Poems*. Lines of earlier versions that have been deleted are given numbers suffixed by *X* to show their position; for example, ll. 29X–32X in the *Fugitive* version of "The Equilibrists" appeared between ll. 28 and 29 of the present version. The order of the poems is alphabetical.

Volumes are abbreviated as follows:

Grace After Meat, 1924: GM
Chills and Fever, 1924: CF
Two Gentlemen in Bonds, 1927: TGB
Fugitives: An Anthology of Verse, 1928: FA
Selected Poems, 1945: SP45
Poems and Essays, 1955: PE
Selected Poems: A Revised and Enlarged Edition, 1963: SP63

Antique Harvesters

A.

1. Tawny are the leaves turned, but they still hold.
2. It is the harvest; what shall this land produce?

7. "I hear the creak of a raven's funeral wing."

21. Under quaint archetypes of chivalry;

28. But grey will quench it shortly—the fields, men, stones.
29. Pluck fast, dreamers; prove as you rumble slowly

31. Bare the arm too, dainty youths, bend the knees

43. True, it is said of our Lady, she ageth.
44. But see, if you peep shrewdly, she hath not stooped;
45. Take no thought of her servitors that have drooped,
46. For we are nothing; and if one talk of death—
47. Why, the ribs of the earth subsist frail as a breath
48. If but God wearieth.

> —*Southwest Review*, X, No. 3 (April, 1925), 13–14

B. (TGB)

1. Tawny are the leaves turned but they still hold,
2. And it is harvest; what shall this land produce?

7. "I hear the croak of a raven's funeral wing."

21. Straddled with archetypes of chivalry;

28. But grey will quench it shortly—the field, men, stones.

31. Bare the arm, dainty youths, bend the knees

(43–48 omitted)

C. (SP45)

29. Pluck fast, dreamers; prove as you amble slowly

(43–48 restored)

Armageddon
A.

9. But Antichrist got down from his Barbary beast

12. And raised him, his own hand about the waist.

13. At first they fingered chivalry's quaint page,

20. Obtuse and most untoward for attack.

24. There stood the white pavilion on the hill.

Nor were they hacked and harried to their boot;
Men die when wounds insufferable are got;
These, plagued with immortality, could not, } 25X–28X
When grim Lord Ares trod them underfoot.

28. But Antichrist ejected small remarks.

31. Then Christ about his adversary's poll
32. Wrapped a dry palm inscribed Mount Calvary.

33. Christ wore a dusty cassock, till the knight

50. The true Heir keeping with the rank impostor;

52. Were strangely jangled with the dithyramb.

56. Betwixt the children of the light and dark.

57. He sought the ear of Christ on these mad things,
58. And, in the white pavilion when he stood
59. And saw them featured and dressed like twins at food,
60. He poured in the wrong ear his misgivings.

66. Christ shed unmannerly his devil's pelf,
67. Took ashes from the hearth and smeared himself,
68. Called for his smock and jennet as before.

71. With stones they whet the axe-heads on the helves,

75. Antichrist and his armies of malfeasance

—*Armageddon*
(Charleston: The Poetry Society
of South Carolina, 1923), pp. 9–12

B. (GM)

9. But Antichrist got down from the Barbary beast

12. And raised him, his own hand about his waist.

20. Inert, and most unusual for attack.

24. And there stood the white pavilion on the hill.

31. The Christ about his adversary's poll

33. Christ wore a dusty cassock, and the knight

56. Between the children of the light and dark.

71. With stone they whet the axe-heads on the helves,

75. Antichrist and the armies of malfeasance

c. (CF)

13. And then they fingered chivalry's quaint page,

20. Obtuse, and most indifferent in attack.

24. There stood the white pavilion on the hill;

28. And Antichrist ejected scant remarks.

31. Then Christ about his adversary's poll

50. The True Heir keeping with the poor Impostor,

52. Were jangled strangely with the dithyramb.

D. (SP45)

12. And raised him, his own hand about the waist.

20. Obtuse, and most indifferent to attack.

(25X–28X deleted)

32. Wrapped a dry palm that grew on Calvary.

E. (PE)

13. Then next they fingered chivalry's quaint page,

57. He sought the ear of Christ on these strange things,
58. But in the white pavilion when he stood,
59. And saw them favored and dressed like twins at food,
60. Profound and mad became his misgivings.

61. The voices, and their burdens, he must hear,
62. But equal between the pleasant Princes flew
63. Theology, the arts, the old customs and the new; } added
64. Hoarsely he ran and hissed in the wrong ear.

66. Christ sheds unmannerly his devil's pelf,
67. Takes ashes from the hearth and smears himself,
68. Calls for his smock and jennet as before.

Blue Girls

A.

(Version A was discarded entirely, so that none of its lines correspond
to those of the present version.)

If I were younger, travelling the bright sward
Under the towers of your seminary,
I should get a look, and a thought, or even a word;
But I am old, and of aspect too contrary
For you who are less weary.

For why do you bind white fillets about your tresses
And weave such stately rhythms where you go?
Why do you whirl so lovingly your blue dresses,
Like haughty bluebirds chattering in the snow
Of what they cannot know?

Practice your beauty, blue girls, if you will;
The lean preceptress, she of history,
Showed you the manifold of good and ill,
And all you saw was princes crooking the knee
To beauteous majesty.

Do you think there are thrones enough, one for each queen?
Some thrones are chairs, some three-legged milking stools,
Or you even sit in ashes where thrones should have been;
And it is for this, God help us all for fools,
You practice in the schools.

Practice your beauty, blue girls, nevertheless;
Once the preceptress, learned bitter one,
Printed the sward in a flounce of purple dress
And was a princess pacing as to her throne;
But now you see she is none.

—*The Fugitive*, III, No. 3 (June, 1924), 82

B. (TGB)

5. Tie the white fillets then about your lustrous hair

C. (SP45)

5. Tie the white fillets then about your hair

Dead Boy

A. THE DEAD BOY

1. The little cousin is gone, by a sad subtraction,

3. And the country kin sit glowering on the transaction,
4. And some of the world of outer dark, like me.

9. A pig with a pasty face, I had long said,
10. Squealing for cakes, and fixing his base pretence
11. On a noble house. But here is the little man dead,
12. And these are the very forbears' lineaments.

19. But it is the old tree's late branch wrenched away,
20. Aggrieving the sapless limbs, all shorn and shaken.

—*The Sewanee Review*, XXXII, No. 2 (April, 1924), 129

B. (TGB)

1. The little cousin is dead, by foul subtraction,

3. And neither the county kin love the transaction
4. Nor some of the world of outer dark, like me.

5. He was not a beautiful boy, nor good, nor clever, ⎫
6. A black cloud full of storms too hot for keeping, ⎬ added
7. A sword beneath his mother's heart,—yet never ⎪
8. Woman bewept her babe as this is weeping. ⎭

9. A pig with a pasty face, I had always said.
10. Squealing for cookies, kinned by pure pretense
11. With a noble house. But the little man quite dead,
12. I can see the forbears' antique lineaments.

19. But this was the old tree's late branch wrenched away,
20. Aggrieving the sapless limbs, the shorn and shaken.

c. (sp45)

3. And none of the county kin like the transaction,

5. A boy not beautiful, nor good, nor clever,

9. A pig with a pasty face, so I had said,
10. Squealing for cookies, kinned by poor pretense

12. I see the forbears' antique lineaments.

20. Grieving the sapless limbs, the shorn and shaken.

Eclogue

A.

9. We were quick-foot the deer, strong-heart the ox,
10. Business-man the bee.

44. Till on one day the face of Death appear—

66. JANE SNEED SAID SLOWLY: I suppose it stands

68. Still wander lovers in the fairy lands
69. Who, when stalks Night the dark and fathomless,

71. And well, John Black, those darkened lovers may,
72. For hands hold much of heat in little storage,
73. And eyes are flickerless torches good as day;
74. The flame of each to the other's flame cries Courage!
75. Soon heart to heart slide they;

76. Thus unafraid they keep the whole night through,
77. Till the sun of a sudden glowing through the brushes,

79. They run to the fields, and apprehend the thrushes,
80. And print the fairy dew.

—*The Fugitive,* IV, No. 1 (March, 1925), 22–24

B. (TGB)

44. Till on one day the dream of Death appear—

C. (SP45)

9. We were quick-foot the deer, strong-back the ox,
10. We were the busy bee.

44. Till in one day the dream of Death appear—

66. JANE SNEED SIGHED SLOWLY: I suppose it stands

68. Still faithful lovers wander in some lands
69. Who when Night stalks, the dark and fathomless,

76. So unafraid they keep the whole night through,
77. Till the sun of a sudden glowing through the bushes

79. They run to the fields, and beautiful the thrushes,
80. Fabulous the dew.

D. (PE)

68. Perhaps there wander lovers in some lands
69. Who when Night comes, when it is fathomless,

71. And well, John Black the darkened lovers may,
72. The hands hold much of heat in little storage,
73. The eyes are almost torches good as day,
74. And one flame to the other flame cries Courage,
75. When heart to heart slide they;

76. So they keep unafraid the whole night through,

79. And listen! are those not the doves, the thrushes?
80. Look there! the golden dew.

Emily Hardcastle, Spinster

A.

2. Bringing not the face of envy, but a gift of praise and lilies

8. We were proper local beauties, and we beautifully trusted
9. If the proud one had to tarry we would take her by default.

10. But right across the threshold has her Grizzled Baron come;
11. Let them wrap her as a princess, who will patter down a stairway,
12. Where the foreigner may take her for his gloomy Halidom.

—The Literary Review, Nov. 3, 1923, p. 201

B. (CF)

2. We shall bring no face of envy, but a gift of praise and lilies

8. We were only local beauties, and we beautifully trusted

10. But right across her threshold has the Grizzled Baron come;
11. Let them wrap her as a princess, who would patter down a stairway

C. (SP45)

9. If the proud one had to tarry we would have her by default.

D. (PE)

10. But right across her threshold has her Grizzled Baron come;
11. Let them wrap her as a princess, who'd go softly down a stairway
12. And seal her to the stranger for his castle in the gloom.

The Equilibrists

A. HISTORY OF TWO SIMPLE LOVERS

6. From whence came heat that flamed upon the kiss,

16. And unsaid: Honor, Honor, they kept crying.

The beauty of their bodies was the bond
Which these incarnate might not pass beyond;
Invincible proud Honor was the bar   29X–32X
Which made them not come closer but stay far.

50. Their flames were no more radiant than their ice.

52. And made these lines to memorize the doom:

—*The Fugitive,* IV, No. 3 (Sept., 1925), 87–88

B. (TGB)

6. From which came heat that flamed upon the kiss,

16. And unsaid: Honor, Honor, they came crying.

(29X–32X deleted)

50. Their flames were not more radiant than their ice.

52. And made these lines to memorize their doom:—

c. (FA)

6. From whence came heat that flamed upon the kiss,

D. (SP45)

6. From which came heat that flamed upon the kiss,

$$Epitaph \left\{ \begin{array}{l} \text{added as heading for} \\ \text{last four lines} \end{array} \right.$$

Good Ships

A.

2. Who speak, and unto eternity diverge—

13. Beautiful timbers meant for stormy sport

—*The Fugitive*, II, No. 9 (Oct., 1923), 131

B. (CF)

13. Beautiful timbers fit for stormy sport

c. (SP45)

2. Who speak, and then unto the vast diverge,

13. Beautiful timbers fit for storm and sport

Hilda

"Hilda" was first printed as a single sonnet titled "Ghosts" in *Harper's Magazine*, CLIV (Dec., 1926), 50, which became without change sonnet II of version A.

A. (TGB)

I

1. The dearest one was she to whom it fell

6. I cast bright flowers, till garlanded she stood

10. I cannot. On the dropping of each petal

11. Rode one that disrespected both the little
12. Bloom and lady; him she was looking at,

14. I was such earth that whispered in her ear.

II

1. The loveliest are perished. And now uprise
2. Ghosts in this garden, that hollow and clamorous

5. The obsequious phantoms and disbodied sighs.

9. O Hilda, proudest of the ladies gone,

14. But flesh hath monstrous gravity, as of stone.

B. (SP63)

I

1. The dearest was the one to whom it fell

6. I brought bright flowers, till garlanded she stood

10. I cannot. On the dropping of those petals
11. Rode the Estranger, scorning their sweet mettles,
12. Blossoms and woman too; him she looked at,

14. I was a clod mumbling, to catch her ear.

II

1. The perished were the fairest. And now uprise
2. Particular ghosts, who hollow and clamorous

5. Obsequious phantoms and disbodied sighs.

9. But Hilda! proudest, lingering last alone,

14. But what I wear is flesh; it weighs like stone.

Janet Waking

A.

10. Running on little pink feet upon the grass

14. Came droning down on Chucky's bald old head

23. (Translated far beyond the prayers of men)

—*The Fugitive*, IV, No. 3 (Sept., 1925), 86

B. (TGB)

14. Came droning down on Chucky's old bald head

23. (Translated far beyond the daughters of men)

C. (SP45)

10. Running across the world upon the grass

Necrological

A.

 2. And scourged his limbs, and afterwards would have slept;

 9. The dead men wore no raiment against the air,
10. Bartholomew's men despoiled them where they fell;
11. In defeat the heroes' bosoms were whitely bare,

17. The lords of chivalry were prone and shattered,

20. The conqueror went to be striken of other foemen.

21. The monastic strode beneath the firmament
22. And found a warrior, clutching whose mighty knees
23. Was a leman, who in her flame had warmed his tent,

30. Deep in the belly of a lugubrious wight;
31. He fingered it well and found it cunningly made,—

33. Then he sat upon a hill and hung his head,
34. Riddling, riddling, and lost in a vast surmise,
35. So still that he likened himself unto those dead

—The Fugitive, I, No. 2 (June, 1922), 62–63

B. (GM)

 2. And scourged his limbs, and afterward would have slept;

10. Bartholomew's men had spoiled them where they fell;

20. Bartholomew went to be stricken of other foemen.

21. Beneath the blue ogive of the firmament
22. Was a dead warrior, clutching whose mighty knees
23. Was a leman, who by her flame had warmed his tent,

34. Riddling, riddling, lost in a vast surmise,

C. (CF)

2. And scourged his limbs, and afterwards would have slept;

23. Was a leman, who with her flame had warmed his tent,

30. Deep in the belly of a lugubrious knight;
31. He fingered it well, and it was cunningly made;

34. Riddling, riddling, and lost in a vast surmise,
35. And so still that he likened himself unto those dead

D. (FA)

30. Deep in the belly of a lugubrious wight.

E. (SP45)

11. In defeat the heroes' bodies were whitely bare,

17. The lords of chivalry lay prone and shattered,

F. (PE)

33. Then he sat upon a hill and bowed his head
34. As under a riddle, and in a deep surmise
35. So still that he likened himself unto those dead

G. (SP63)

9. The dead wore no raiment against the air,

Of Margaret

A. AUTUMN GRIEF OF MARGARET

1. At the fall of the first leaf that wind rends
2. She and the bough tremble, and she will mourn

4. But with louder destruction the wind sounds.

5. Soon these all will decline who heavy hang
6. In gelid air, and the blind land be filled
7. With dead, and but a windiness unchild

10. And, behind that, conception; hers was large,

14. All her generations were of the head,
15. The eyes begot but not the wishful blood
16. And the issue was but flowers and foliage.

17. Virgin, whose image tall in the green grass
18. I keep, you are acquit of statute wrong;
19. And let the maiden pageant ever sing
20. Of this far away time of gentleness.

—*The Saturday Review of Literature,* Sept. 29, 1934, p. 137

B. (SP45)

1. With the fall of the first leaf that winds rend
2. She and the boughs trembled, and she would mourn

4. But with louder destruction sang the wind.

5. Soon must they all descend, there where they hung

7. With dead, and a mere windiness unchild

14. For her generations were of the head,
15. The eyes, the tender fingers, not the blood,
16. And the issue was all flowers and foliage.

17. Virgin, whose image bent to the small grass
18. I keep against this tide of wayfaring,
19. O hear the maiden pageant ever sing
20. Of that far away time of gentleness.

C. (PE)

5. So must the others drop, there where they hung
6. Quaking and cold, and the blind land be filled
7. With dead, till one least and last wind unchild

Old Mansion
A.

2. To mask decently a quite meddlesome stare,

8. Reiterations which gentle readers abhor

Each time of seeing, I absorbed some other feature
Of a house whose legend could in no wise be brief
Nor ignoble; for it expired as sweetly as Nature,
With her tinge of oxidation on autumn leaf.   } 9X–12X

9. It was a Southern manor. One need hardly imagine
10. Towers, white monoliths, or even ivied walls;
11. But sufficient state if its peacock *was* a pigeon;
12. Where no courts held, but grave rites and funerals.

20. Green blinds dragging frightened the watchful heart

22. Its exits and entrances suiting the children of men,

28. Or crumbs of history dropping from their full store.

30. Which has been deplored duly with a beating of the breast.

35. Than that warped concierge and imperturbable vassal
36. Who bids you begone from her master's Gothic park.

39. But no annalist went in to the lord or the peons;
40. The antiquary would gather the bits of shard.

42. How loving from my foreign weed the feather curled

—*The Fugitive*, III, No. 2 (April, 1924), 40–41

B. (CF)

Of a house whose annals in no wise could be brief} 10X.

12. Where no courts kept, but grave rites and funerals.

28. Or the crumbs of legend dropping from their great store.

40. The antiquary would finger the bits of shard.

C. (SP45)

2. To mask in decency a meddlesome stare,

28. Or crumbs of legend dropping from their great store.

30. Which has been deplored with a beating of the breast

39. And no annalist went in to the lords or the peons;

D. (PE)

35. Than that wrapped concierge and imperturbable vassal

E. (SP63)

8. Reiterations that gentle readers abhor.

(9X–12X deleted)

9. It was a Southern manor. One hardly imagines
10. Towers, arcades, or forbidding fortress walls;
11. But sufficient state though its peacocks now were pigeons;

20. Green shutters dragging frightened the watchful heart

22. Its porches and bowers suiting the children of men,

28. Or crumbs of wisdom dropping from their great store.

35. Than that warped concierge and imperturbable vassal
36. Who had bid me begone from her master's Gothic park.

42. How loving from my dying weed the feather curled

Painted Head

A.

17. So that the extravagant device of art

22. For vinegar disparagement of flesh

29. The increase of body. Beauty is of body.

—*The New Republic,* Dec. 26, 1934, p. 185

B. (SP45)

22. For having vinegarly traduced the flesh

C. (SP63)

17. Wherefore the extravagant device of art

29. The being of body. Beauty is of body.

Philomela

A.

4. Ah, but our numbers are less felicitous,

13. She wanders when he sits heavy on his roost,

20. To an hypermuscular race?

37. I have despaired if we may make us worthy,
38. This bantering breed sophistical and earthy;

—*The Fugitive,* II, No. 3 (Feb.–March, 1923), 8–9

B. AN AMERICAN ADDRESSES PHILOMELA (GM)

4. Ah, but our numbers are not felicitous,

13. She wanders while he sits heavy on his roost,

37. I have despaired of thee and am unworthy,
38. My scene is prose, this people and I are earthy;

C. (CF)

13. She wanders when he sits heavy on his roost,

20. To an inordinate race?

37. I am in despair if we may make us worthy,
38. A bantering breed sophistical and swarthy;

Prelude to an Evening

(A poem revised and explicated: the soliloquy of a man returning home to his wife)

A. PRELUDE TO AN EVENING: A POEM REVISED AND EXPLICATED

10. Are monstrous only in the dreams

18. If surely cry, cock-crow or bell

21. But now, by our confirmed supposal,
22. Apparition waits upon sunny mornings;
23. You in your peignoir dividing the oranges;
24. But gathering its strength in the shadowed places

25. Invisible evil, deprived and bold.
26. The day-long clock will metronome
27. Your gallant fear; the needles clicking;

31. You shall be listening for a low wind,
32. And the warning sibilance of pines.

—*The Kenyon Review*, XXV, No. 1 (Winter, 1963), 70–71

B. (SP63)

5. You are my scholar. Then languish, expire
6. With each day's terror and next week's doom
7. Till we're twice espoused, in love and ruin,   } added
8. And grave but smiling though the heavens fall.

10. Were monstrous only in the dreams

18. If quickly cry, cock-crow or bell

21. And now? To confirm our strange supposal,
22. Apparitions wait upon sunny mornings;
23. You in your peignoir commend the heaped oranges
24. Gold on the platter for cheeky children

25. But freeze at the turbulence under the floor
26. Where unclean spirits yawn and thrash;
27. The day-long clock will strike your fears;

31. You listen for a low lost wind to awaken
32. The warning sibilance of pines.

Spectral Lovers

A.

1. They walked, they haunted a thicket of April mist,
2. As out of the rich ground strangely come to birth,
3. Else two immaculate angels fallen on earth.

5. Why should two lovers be frozen asunder in fear?

8. Her thrilling fingers touched him quick with care;
9. Of many delicate postures she cast her snare;
10. But for all the red heart beating in the pale bosom,
11. Her face as of cunningly tinctured ivory

12. Was hard with an agony.

13. Stormed by the little batteries of an April night,
14. Passionate being the essences of the field,
15. Should the penetrable walls of the crumbling prison yield?

17. "This is the mad moon, and must I surrender all?

19. And gesturing largely to the very moon of Easter,

21. And beheading some field-flowers that had come to pass,

33. Two clad in the shapes of angels, being spectral lovers,
34. Trailing a glory of moon-gold and amethyst,

—The Fugitive, II, No. 7 (June–July, 1923), 68

B. (CF)

1. By night they haunted a thicket of April mist,

5. Why should two lovers go frozen asunder in fear?

9. Of many delicate postures she cast a snare;

C. (SP45)

2. Out of that black ground suddenly come to birth,
3. Else angels lost in each other and fallen on earth.

5. Why should two lovers go frozen apart in fear?

8. Scarcely her fingers touched him, quick with care,
9. Yet of evasions even she made a snare.
10. The heart was bold that clanged within her bosom,
11. The moment perfect, the time stopped for them,
12. Still her face turned from him.

13. Strong were the batteries of the April night
14. And the stealthy emanations of the field;
15. Should the walls of her prison undefended yield

17. "This is the mad moon, and shall I surrender all?

19. And gesturing largely to the moon of Easter,

21. Beheading some field-flowers that had come to pass,

33. Two tall and wandering, like spectral lovers,
34. White in the season's moon-gold and amethyst,

The Tall Girl

A. ADA RUEL

3. And, when she had caught up even with them, nodded:

7. And we'll walk by the windows where the young men are working

9. But the Queen of Heaven who had advanced and stood
10. In the likeness, I hear, of a fine motherly woman

—The Fugitive, III, No. 2 (April, 1924), 39

B. (CF)

3. And, when she was caught up even with them, nodded:

9. But the Queen of Heaven on the other side of the road

C. (SP45)

7. And we'll go by the windows where the young men are working

10. In the likeness, I hear, of a plain motherly woman

Vaunting Oak

A.

1. He is a tower unleaning. But he may break
2. If Heaven in a rage try him too windily;
3. And what uproar tall towers concumbent make:

5. Of timeless trunk that is too vast to shake;
6. Only the temporal twigs are abashed on their seat,

8. Of the mad humours of wind, and turn and beat
9. Ecstatic around the stem on which they are captive.

But he casts the feeble generations of leaf,
And naked to the spleen of the cold skies eruptive
That howl on his defiant head in chief,   } 10X–
                                                       15X
Bears out their frenzy to its period,
And hears in the spring, a little more rheumy and deaf,
After the tragedy the lyric palinode. . . .

11. Yoked with an unbeliever of bitter blood,

13. And she exulted—being given to crying,
14. "Heart, Heart, love is so firm an entity,
15. It must not go the way of the hot rose dying"—

16. For the venerable oak, delivered of his pangs
17. Put forth his flames of green with profuse joying

19. And what but she fetch me up to the steep place
20. Where the oak vaunted? A meadow of many songs

22. Of daisies, and yellow kinds; and here she knew,
23. Who had sorely been instructed of much decease,

25. But above the little and their dusty tombs was he
26. Standing, sheer on his hill, soiled by few
27. Of the knobs and broken boughs of an old tree,

28. And she murmured, "He is established you see forever."
29. But thinking that she had lied too piteously,

32. "Largely, the old gentleman is," I grieved, "cadaver.
33. Before our joy shall have lapsed, even, he is gone."

35. Boomed till its round reverberance had outdone

39. Or the tears of a girl discovering her dread.

                    —*The Fugitive*, II, No. 10 (Dec., 1923), 174–175

B. ILEX PRISCUS (GM)

9. Ecstatic round the stem to which they are captive.

17. Put forth his flames of green in profuse joying

19. And who but she fetched me up to the steep place

22. Of daisies and yellow kinds; whereof she knew,

C. (CF)

9. Ecstatic around the stem on which they are captive.

17. Put forth his flames of green with profuse joying

19. And what but she fetch me up to the steep place

22. Of daisies, and yellow kinds; and here she knew

39. Or the tears of a girl remembering her dread.

D. (SP45)

1. He is a tower unleaning. But how will he not break,
2. If Heaven assault him with full wind and sleet,
3. And what uproar tall trees concumbent make!

5. Naked he rears against the cold skies eruptive;
6. Only his temporal twigs are unsure of seat,

8. Of the mad humors of wind, and turn and flee
9. In panic round the stem on which they are captive.

(10X–15X deleted)

11. Linked with an unbeliever of bitter blood,

13. And exulted, wrapped in a phantasy of good:
14. "Be the great oak for its long winterings
15. Our love's symbol, better than the summer's brood."

16. Then the venerable oak, delivered of his pangs,
17. Put forth profuse his green banners of peace

20. Where the oak vaunted? A flat where birdsong flew

23. Who had been instructed of much mortality,

25. Above the little and their dusty tombs was he
26. Standing, sheer on his hill, not much soiled over
27. By the knobs and broken boughs of an old tree,

28. And she murmured, "Established, you see him there! forever."
29. But, that her pitiful error be undone,

32. "The old gentleman," I grieved, "holds gallantly,
33. But before our joy shall have lapsed, even, will be gone."

35. Boomed till its loud reverberance outsounded

What Ducks Require

A.

7. This zone is temperate. The pond,

11. On a cold spring ground and render
12. A space supportable, and a time tender.

17. Planting dangerous at the earth-heart
18. Where warm and cold precisely start.

20. And, O lewd fox and fowler's ear,
21. The epithalamion unsung:—
22. Web-toes of progeny appear,
23. Cold-hatched, and from the blink of birth
24. Suckle the sweet cold breast of earth.

25. The prodigious duck makes melodies
26. You have not learned, pale scholars: low

—*The New Republic*, April 27, 1927, p. 273

B. (FA)

17. Planting dangerous by the earth-heart

20. From the lewd fox and fowler's eye
21. Till, in that dim sequestering,
22. Webtoed the lustrous progeny
23. Is coldhatched, and from the blink of birth
24. Suckles the sweet cold breast of earth.

Ridiculously born he is} 25X added
25. Unto prodigious melodies

C. (SP45)

17. Planting dangerous at the earth-heart

20. From the lewd eye and fowler's gun
21. Till in that wet sequestering,
22. Webtoed, the progeny is done,
23. Cold-hatched, and from the blink of birth
24. Is native to the rhythmed earth.

(25X deleted)
25. Prodigious in his wide degrees
26. Who, as the winds and waters blow,

D. (PE)

7. The zone unready. But the pond,

11. On a cold spring ground, a freak,
12. A weathering chance even in the wrack.

17. The marsh quakes dangerous, the port
18. Where wet and dry precisely start.

23. Cold-hatched, the infant prodigy tries
24. To preen his feathers for the skies.

26. Who where the winds and waters blow

Winter Remembered

A. (AN ENGLISH SONNET)

8. Far from my cause, my proper heat, my centre.

9. Better to walk forth in the murderous air

13. Which would you choose, and for what boot in gold,
14. The absence, or the absence and the cold?

—*The Sewanee Review*, XXX, No. 1 (Jan., 1922), 1

B. (GM)

My winter's leave was much too cold for smarting.
What bitter winds, and numbing snows and sorrows,
And wheezy pines, like old men undeparting,
To funeralize against all green young morrows!

} 5X–8X added

8. Far from my cause, my proper heat and centre.

13. And where I went, the hugest winter blast
14. Would have this body bowed, these eyeballs streaming,
15. And though I think this heart's blood froze not fast,
16. It ran too small to spare one drop for dreaming.

17. Dear love, these fingers that had known your touch
18. And tied our separate forces first together,
19. Were ten poor idiot fingers not worth much,
20. Ten frozen parsnips hanging in the weather!

} added

C. (CF)

(5X–8X deleted)

D. (PE)

9. Better to walk forth in the frozen air

13. And where I walked, the murderous winter blast

Selected Bibliography

Books

Bradbury, John M. *The Fugitives: A Critical Account.* Chapel Hill: The University of North Carolina Press, 1958.

Brooks, Cleanth. *Modern Poetry and the Tradition.* Chapel Hill: The University of North Carolina Press, 1939.

————, et al. *Conversations on the Craft of Poetry.* ("A transcript of the tape recording made to accompany *Understanding Poetry,* Third Edition.") New York: Holt, Rinehart, and Winston, 1961.

Cowan, Louise. *The Fugitive Group: A Literary History.* Baton Rouge: Louisiana State University Press, 1959.

Davidson, Donald. *Southern Writers in the Modern World.* ("Eugenia Dorothy Blount Lamar Memorial Lectures," 1957.) Athens: University of Georgia Press, 1958.

Gregory, Horace, and Marya Zaturenska. *A History of American Poetry: 1900–1940.* New York: Harcourt, Brace and Co., 1946.

Gross, Harvey. *Sound and Form in Modern Poetry.* Ann Arbor: The University of Michigan Press, 1964.

Knight, Karl F. *The Poetry of John Crowe Ransom.* ("Studies in American Literature," II.) The Hague: Mouton and Co., 1964.

Ostroff, Anthony (ed.). *The Contemporary Poet as Artist and Critic: Eight Symposia.* Boston: Little, Brown and Co., 1964.

Purdy, Rob Roy (ed.). *Fugitives' Reunion: Conversations at Vanderbilt, May 3–5, 1956.* Nashville: Vanderbilt University Press, 1959.

Riding, Laura, and Robert Graves. *A Survey of Modernist Poetry.* Garden City, N. Y.: Doubleday, Doran and Co., Inc., 1928.

Rubin, Louis D., and Robert D. Jacobs (eds.). *South: Modern Southern Literature in its Cultural Setting.* Garden City, N. Y.: Doubleday and Co., Inc., 1961.

Stewart, John L. *The Burden of Time: The Fugitives and Agrarians.* Princeton, N. J.: Princeton University Press, 1965.

153

————. *John Crowe Ransom.* ("University of Minnesota Pamphlets on American Writers," No. 18.) Minneapolis: University of Minnesota Press, 1962.

Tate, Allen. *Collected Essays.* Denver: Alan Swallow, 1959.

Winters, Yvor. *In Defense of Reason.* Denver: Alan Swallow, 1947.

Articles and Periodicals

Beatty, Richmond Croom. "John Crowe Ransom as Poet," *The Sewanee Review,* LII, No. 3 (Summer, 1944), 344–366.

Beloof, Robert. "Strength in the Exquisite: A Study of John Crowe Ransom's Prosody," *Annali Istituto Universitario Orientale, Napoli, Sezione Germanica,* IV (1961), 215–222.

Bergonzi, Bernard. "A Poem About the History of Love," *Critical Quarterly,* IV, No. 2 (Summer, 1962), 127–137.

Bleifuss, William. "Ransom's 'Here Lies a Lady,'" *The Explicator,* XI, No. 7 (May, 1953), Item 51.

Booth, Philip. "Ransom's Dedication to 'What Poetry Is and What Poetry Can Be,'" *The Christian Science Monitor,* Aug. 1, 1963, p. 11.

Brooks, Cleanth. "The Doric Delicacy," *The Sewanee Review,* LVI, No. 3 (Summer, 1948), 402–415.

————. "The Modern Southern Poet and Tradition," *The Virginia Quarterly Review,* XI, No. 2 (April, 1935), 305–320.

Carne-Ross, D. S. "Ransom's 'Judith of Bethulia,'" *Nine,* II, No. 2 (May, 1950), 91–95.

Eberhart, Richard. "The Search for Perfection," *Poetry,* LXVII, No. 4 (Jan., 1946), 212–215.

Fraser, G. S. "Ransom Revised," *The New York Review of Books,* Oct. 31, 1963, pp. 8–9.

Gamble, Isabel. "Ceremonies of Bravery: John Crowe Ransom," *Hopkins Review,* VI (Spring–Summer, 1953), 105–115.

Graves, Robert. "Muscular Poetry," *The Saturday Review of Literature,* Dec. 27, 1924, p. 412.

Grigson, Geoffrey. "John Crowe Ransom," *New Verse,* No. 16 (Aug.–Sept., 1935), pp. 12–17.

Heilman, Robert B. "Poetic and Prosaic: Program Notes on Opposite Numbers," *The Pacific Spectator,* V, No. 4 (Autumn, 1951), 454–463.

Hough, Graham. "John Crowe Ransom: The Poet and the Critic," *The Southern Review*, I, New Series, No. 1 (Jan., 1965), 1–21.

———. "Marvell of the Deep South," *The Listener*, Aug. 4, 1960, pp. 183–185.

Jarrell, Randall. "John Crowe Ransom's Poetry," *The Sewanee Review*, LVI, No. 3 (Summer, 1948), 378–390.

Koch, Vivienne. "The Achievement of John Crowe Ransom," *The Sewanee Review*, LVIII, No. 2 (Spring, 1950), 227–261.

Mason, Ellsworth. "Ransom's 'Here Lies a Lady,'" *The Explicator*, VIII, No. 1 (Oct., 1949), Item 1.

Matthiessen, F. O. "American Poetry: 1920–40," *The Sewanee Review*, LV, No. 1 (Winter, 1947), 24–55.

———. "Primarily Language," *The Sewanee Review*, LVI, No. 3 (Summer, 1948), 391–401.

Nemerov, Howard. "Summer's Flare and Winter's Flaw," *The Sewanee Review*, LVI, No. 3 (Summer, 1948), 416–425.

Parsons, Thornton H. "The Civilized Poetry of John Crowe Ransom," *Perspective*, XIII, No. 4 (Autumn, 1964), 244–262.

———. "Ransom and the Poetics of Monastic Ecstasy," *Modern Language Quarterly*, XXVI, No. 4 (Dec., 1965), 571–585.

———. "Ransom the Revisionist," *The Southern Review*, II, New Series, No. 2 (Spring, 1966), 453–463.

Peck, Virginia L. "Ransom's 'Prelude to an Evening,'" *The Explicator*, XX, No. 5 (Jan., 1962), Item 41.

Rubin, Louis D. "John Ransom's Cruell Battle," *Shenandoah*, IX, No. 1 (Winter, 1958), 23–35.

Schwartz, Elias. "Ransom's 'Bells for John Whiteside's Daughter,'" *English Language Notes*, I, No. 4 (June, 1964), 284–285.

Spencer, Theodore. "Distinguished Talent," *The Saturday Review of Literature*, July 14, 1945, pp. 30–31.

Stauffer, Donald A. "Portrait of the Critic-Poet as Equilibrist," *The Sewanee Review*, LVI, No. 3 (Summer, 1948), 426–434.

Stocking, Fred H. "Ransom's 'Here Lies a Lady,'" *The Explicator*, VIII, No. 1 (Oct., 1949), Item 1.

Tate, Allen. "The Eighteenth-Century South," *The Nation*, March 30, 1927, p. 346.

———. "For John Crowe Ransom at Seventy-five," *Shenandoah*, XIV, No. 3 (Spring, 1963), 5–8.

———. "The Fugitive, 1922–25," *Princeton University Library Chronicle*, III, No. 3 (April, 1942), 75–84.

Wallach, Virginia. "Ransom's 'Painted Head,' " *The Explicator*, XIV, No. 7 (April, 1956), Item 45.

Warren, Robert Penn. "John Crowe Ransom: A Study in Irony," *The Virginia Quarterly Review*, XI, No. 1 (Jan., 1935), 93–112.

————. "A Note on Three Southern Poets," *Poetry*, XL, No. 2 (May, 1932), 103–113.

————. "Pure and Impure Poetry," *The Kenyon Review*, V, No. 2 (Spring, 1943), 228–254.

Wasserman, G. R. "The Irony of John Crowe Ransom," *The University of Kansas City Review*, XXIII, No. 2 (Winter, 1956), 151–160.

Williamson, George. "Donne and the Poetry of Today," in *A Garland for John Donne: 1631–1931*, ed. Theodore Spencer (Gloucester, Mass.: Peter Smith, 1958), pp. 153–176.

Index